Windows Netbooks

The Path to Low-Cost Computing

■ ■ ■

James Floyd Kelly

Apress®

Windows Netbooks: The Path to Low-Cost Computing

Copyright © 2009 by James Floyd Kelly

ISBN-13 (pbk): 978-1-4302-2399-3

ISBN-13 (electronic): 978-1-4302-2400-6

Lead Editor: Frank Pohlmann
Technical Reviewer: Mary Ann C. Tan
Editorial Board: Clay Andres, Steve Anglin, Mark Beckner, Ewan Buckingham, Tony Campbell, Gary Cornell, Jonathan Gennick, Michelle Lowman, Matthew Moodie, Jeffrey Pepper, Frank Pohlmann, Ben Renow-Clarke, Dominic Shakeshaft, Matt Wade, Tom Welsh
Project Manager: Sofia Marchant
Copy Editor: Patrick Meader
Associate Production Director: Kari Brooks-Copony
Production Editor: Kelly Winquist
Compositor: Diana Van Winkle
Proofreader: Kim Burton
Indexer: Becky Hornyak
Artist: April Milne
Cover Designer: Jerry Votta
Manufacturing Director: Tom Debolski

Distributed to the book trade worldwide by Springer-Verlag New York, Inc., 233 Spring Street, 6th Floor, New York, NY 10013. Phone 1-800-SPRINGER, fax 201-348-4505, e-mail orders-ny@springer-sbm.com, or visit http://www.springeronline.com.

For information on translations, please contact Apress directly at 2855 Telegraph Avenue, Suite 600, Berkeley, CA 94705. Phone 510-549-5930, fax 510-549-5939, e-mail info@apress.com, or visit http://www.apress.com.

Apress and friends of ED books may be purchased in bulk for academic, corporate, or promotional use. eBook versions and licenses are also available for most titles. For more information, reference our Special Bulk Sales–eBook Licensing web page at http://www.apress.com/info/bulksales.

For Ashley and Decker

Contents at a Glance

Contents

About the Author

JAMES FLOYD KELLY, a freelance writer living in Atlanta, Georgia, has degrees in English and Industrial Engineering. A long-time LEGO MINDSTORMS developer, he is editor-in-chief of the world's most popular LEGO blog, *thenxtstep.com*, which continues to draw an estimated 40,000+ readers monthly. James is also a regular beta tester for the LEGO MINDSTORMS development team. His most recent books include *Don't Spend a Dime: The Path to Low-Cost Computing* and *Ubuntu on a Dime*. He enjoys spending time with his wife and two-year-old son, who has yet to show any real interest in computers despite his dad slipping a netbook into the little guy's bed at night.

About the Technical Reviewer

 **MARY ANN C. TAN** has experience in many fields, including slinging regular expressions, watching Linux servers, writing telecom billing systems, arguing about machine learning, and being an obsessive-compulsive spreadsheet user. She is learning Italian, has forgotten most of her Mandarin, trains cats using Cat-Kwan-Do, and sings videoke to survive the Manila nights. She currently does GUI development for a telecom testing company as her day job.

Acknowledgments

Thanking those involved in bringing a book to fruition never gets old. I am extremely fortunate to have worked with some great people during the writing of this book: Dominic Shakeshaft, Jonathan Gennick, Sofia Marchant, Patrick Meader, Jeff Pepper, Jerry Votta, Becky Hornyak, Diana Van Winkle, Kim Burton, and Kelly Winquist. Thank you, one and all, for your assistance and support on this book.

My wife, Ashley, also gets a huge Thank You for her support and patience. She always forgives me for those moments of pure panic when deadlines start to loom, and I start acting a little crazy. I wrote two other books for Apress simultaneously with this one, which exacerbated my level of craziness tremendously. So, while I'd like to make a public promise to my wife that I will never do that again, let's just say I will *try* to not to put myself in this situation again...

Introduction

I think netbooks are here to stay. Let me tell you why. About a year ago I went out for lunch to a local Chinese food restaurant. While I was eating, I saw a sign on the wall that said, "Free WiFi." I know that some Chik-fil-A restaurants have free WiFi (and my office-away-from-the-office, Atlanta Bread Company, does too), but this struck me as funny while I was eating an eggroll. Then my mobile phone rang—a friend wanted to know if I could quickly review a resume he'd emailed me for a job interview he was scheduled for in an hour. I didn't have my laptop with me because I hated to lug that thing around when I was just going out for lunch. I shoveled my food quickly, so I could drive back to my home office and look his resume over.

Things would be different if this happened today. I rarely leave my home office without toting along my new netbook. I typically carry it like a small hardback book, with no case, no power cord, and no extra devices. It's just my netbook and me. I can get away with this because WiFi is everywhere—even in Chinese restaurants. And based on the number of people I see with their own laptops and netbooks in my favorite haunts (a coffee shop, a bookstore, a few restaurants, and even a cupcake store I've just discovered), WiFi and Internet access seem to be things we all want and have come to expect these days.

Just as I once got used to carrying a mobile phone, I've now gotten used to carrying around my netbook everywhere I go. I don't want to debate the pros and cons of our modern digital lifestyle, but I have to admit it's nice to have this little device with me when I need to check email, check the weather, look at a movie schedule, or order a pair of my favorite Converse All-Star Chucks in black leather (which I just did—thank you, netbook!).

My goal isn't to run complex software on this little machine. I write books, I use the Internet to research stuff, and I email friends and family. Ninety percent of what I do with my netbook happens in a web browser! I spent about $300 on the netbook itself, and I haven't spent another dime on any software for it. For me, this netbook is all about leveraging "the cloud" (see Chapter 3 if you don't know what I'm talking about). I don't want to install software—I just want to use the device when I need it and forget about it when I'm done. Cloud computing is all the rage, and after finishing this book, I'll think you'll see and understand why I'm such a fan, especially for notebooks.

Yes, netbooks are here to stay. The screen and keyboard are smaller than you find on traditional laptops, but the device weighs two pounds, and the battery seems to last me all day because I simply close the lid and put it into hibernation when I'm not using it. What's not to love about that? I'm also seeing these devices everywhere I go, so I think others are finding these low-priced and portable devices as handy as I do.

Skeptical? That's understandable. But that's why I'm hoping you'll read this book and discover how an inexpensive netbook running Windows can be just as useful as its bigger laptop and desktop computing cousins.

Now it's time for lunch. I'm packing up my netbook that I used to write this introduction, and I'm going to head over to this new little pizzeria that's been advertising calzones and free WiFi.

CHAPTER 1

■■■

The Netbook

I love my netbook. It is my favorite tool for accessing the Internet, checking email, listening to music, and, in this instance, writing books. My netbook reminds me of my mobile phone: I often feel lost when I'm not carrying either device around.

I also own a two-year-old laptop (some call them notebooks) and a four-month-old desktop computer. My laptop runs Windows XP Professional and weighs nine pounds, not counting the power supply, blank DVDs, pens, and other stuff crammed into its carrying case. I built the desktop computer myself by purchasing all the components separately; I use each of these computers for different reasons, but I find myself reaching more and more for my netbook. It weighs 2.2 pounds and provides me with three or more hours of battery life before I need to charge it. If someone had told me a year ago that I would be giving up Boat Anchor (what I lovingly call my laptop), I would have laughed out loud. Give up my laptop? Are you crazy? It's how I make a living! Plus I tend to frequent the coffee shops and restaurants that provide free WiFi Internet access and lugging a desktop computer to these places isn't feasible—it's just silly looking. (And I've seen people do it, I kid you not!)

But in February 2009, I found myself looking at new computers in a local technology store when my eyes fell on a collection of small devices that I hadn't seen before. Larger than a mobile phone but smaller than any standard laptop computer I'd ever used, the netbook represented a new category of computing device.

I picked up each netbook. The devices were very light! I brought up various web sites that I frequent and evaluated how the sites appeared on the devices' small screens—not bad! I opened an empty text document and typed away, trying to decide if my typing speed would suffer—for some tasks, yes; for others, no. I looked at everything—the touchpad, USB ports, expansion slots, software, battery life, memory, hard drive size, and warranties—because, hey, it's very likely I'd drop something this small.

I went home, did some more research on the Internet checking descriptions and prices, made a checklist of the things I wanted, and narrowed down the selection. And then I made my purchase. I couldn't be happier. (Figure 1-1 shows Boat Anchor and my new netbook, playing together happily on my desk with my Ubuntu PC's keyboard, mouse, and monitor.)

Figure 1-1. *I didn't have to free up much room on my desktop for my new netbook.*

There are all sorts of questions you might have right now. What is a netbook? Isn't a netbook really just a laptop? Are netbooks actually usable, given their tiny size? Is this just a marketing gimmick to get me to buy a new computer? I'm sure you have other questions, as well, and I'll do my best to answer them.

This chapter is all about defining what *is* and *is not* a netbook. Maybe you've already purchased one and want to learn more about its components. Maybe you're looking for information to help you decide whether a netbook is the device for you. Or maybe you've already decided to buy a netbook but are overwhelmed by all the new choices available. Whatever your reasons for considering a netbook, this chapter should help you answer the many questions that a new type of computing device inevitably raises.

A Netbook Checklist

If you haven't yet purchased a netbook or even decided whether a netbook would meet your needs, then this section is for you. (If you already own a netbook, feel free to skip to Chapter 2.) I'm going to provide you with a checklist (see Figure 1-2) that can help you answer two big questions:

- Should I purchase a netbook?

- If I purchase a netbook, what do I need?

If you find after reading this chapter that a netbook really isn't for you, feel free to donate this book to your local library; the remaining chapters in the book will probably not be of much interest to you. But if this chapter does whet your appetite for a netbook, the provided checklist should help assist you in your search for the netbook that best fits your needs.

Each row in the checklist contains an item that is discussed in the chapter's remaining sections. For each item (row), place a check in the "Need" column if you find that you must have that specific item and a check in the "Nice" column if you'd like that item, but it's not a deal breaker when it comes to your dream netbook. Finally, place a check in the "No Thanks" column if you determine that an item isn't required for you to enjoy a netbook. You can also use the "Notes" column to define your requirements further; for example, in the Hard Drive row, you can enter in a value for the storage capacity you are looking for in your netbook, such as 60 gigabytes or the type of drive.

Note Some items already have a check in the Need column—there are a few things that every computer, no matter the size, must have. You'll need a screen, for example, but use the Notes column to define what screen size you want or need.

You might also find it helpful to visit a nearby store that sells netbooks. This will help you when it comes to issues such as weight, keyboard size, and screen size. Nothing beats being able to pick up various netbooks and compare their weight and other attributes. This hands-on experience can help you further refine your checklist.

Item	Need	Nice	No Thanks	
Screen	✓			Size Desired:
Keyboard	✓			
Touchpad				
Web Cam				
Speakers				
Network Adapter - Ethernet				
USB				How many ports?
Color				
Misc. Ports				
Processor	✓			
Hard Drive - SSD?	✓			Type? Capacity?
Memory - Maximum?	✓			Desired? Maximum?
Operating System	✓			
WiFi Adapter				

Figure 1-2. *This checklist can help you determine the right netbook features for you or even whether a netbook makes sense for you in the first place.*

Netbooks on the Outside

Let's begin by examining a netbook's external features. These include the netbook's screen size, keyboard size, available plugs and ports, and its overall weight. Each of these will be covered in more detail later in this chapter.

If you've never used a laptop before, the netbook's size and weight might not be as big a shock to you as it is to those of us who've had to lug around one of its larger cousins. The screen sizes, however, might come as a shock (probably to anyone under age 25). The screens are small. Sizes typically range from seven inches to 11 inches (measured diagonally). Most netbook displays support extremely fine resolutions, but again, you'll be in a much better position to judge what you need by finding a local netbook seller and examining, not just a given netbook's weight and screen size/resolution, but all of the features described in this chapter.

The features described in this chapter are *not* ranked in order of importance. That said, during your research you'll probably find that one or more of these features will become more important to you than others. That's to be expected.

■**Tip** You'll find that many netbook manufacturers sell almost identical models that differ in only one or two features. (For example, I found two versions of the HP Mini 1033 for sale—the only difference between the two versions was that one had a built-in 10/100 network card, and the other did not. All other hardware was identical, and both had a built-in wireless network card.)

Footprint

A netbook's footprint is simply its overall dimensions: length, width, and thickness. Although the definition of "netbook" has not yet been officially defined by any organization, the general consensus is that netbooks are typically under 13 inches in length and eight inches in width. Height, or thickness, for most netbooks currently available for sale seems to be less than 1.5 inches. Figure 1-3 shows my netbook's length, width, and height. (Be sure to take a look at Appendix A, which provides a list of many netbook manufacturers.)

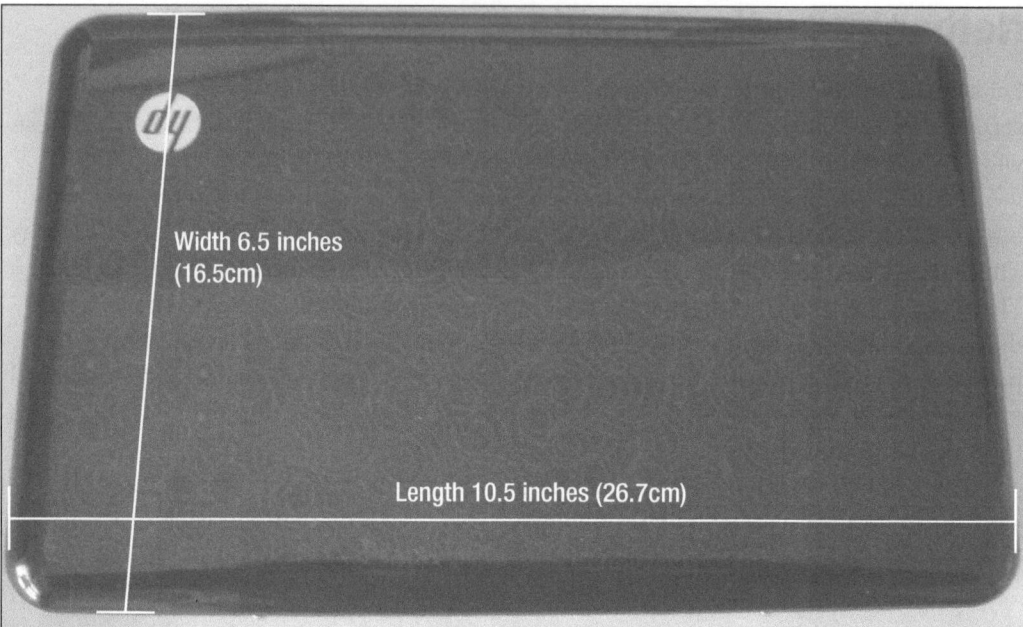

Figure 1-3. *My netbook is fairly typical in terms of length and width.*

Keep in mind that factors that affect a netbook's footprint include its screen size (a larger screen requires a larger lid) and its keyboard size. Other items that can increase a netbook's dimensions include special hardware such as a built-in CD/DVD drive, a larger capacity battery (like a six-cell) or even a touchpad (more on that shortly).

If you're unable to visit a local store that sells netbooks to look at the various sizes available, one option is to simply grab a ruler, draw a rectangle on a piece of cardboard that represents the length and width of any netbook you might be interested in purchasing, and cut it out and compare. It might seem a little strange, but if you're unable to hold a netbook physically, simulating a netbook's footprint can at least give you an idea about the netbook's length and width, as well as let you compare small netbooks to larger netbooks.

It's a bit humorous to refer to netbooks as "a small netbook" or "a large netbook," but I hope you understand my point. Netbooks are small, yes, but even so they come in a variety of sizes and shapes (and colors—my tech editor has a pink one!). My final suggestion to you regarding a netbook's footprint is to let other factors guide you to the proper footprint size. Screen size will have the largest effect, of course, but after you've completed your checklist, you'll have a better understanding of the various factors that affect a netbook's size and functionality, and you can make your decision accordingly.

Weight

My HP Mini netbook weighs a little over two pounds (or one kilogram). Most netbooks seem to fall between two pounds and four pounds, but new netbooks are appearing every month, and I expect the weights at the lower and upper ends to go lower and higher, respectively.

Weight is one of those attributes that is extremely subjective. One person tells me my netbook is light, and another picks it up and tells me it's fairly heavy "for a netbook." All I can suggest to you at this point is to go pick up a few netbooks and judge them for yourself. If a salesman will let you, arrange them from lightest to heaviest and write down the weights on your checklist. Be sure to include any cables and extras you plan on carrying with you. Go with your gut instinct on this one and write in a maximum weight on your checklist that you would be willing to put up with when carrying your netbook. (I frequently carry my netbook by itself—no bag and no power cord. It looks like a small hardback book and that's how I carry it.)

Tip Keep in mind when doing research that the weight of the netbook is typically listed with the battery installed. I have a sneaky feeling that some manufacturers may start shipping netbooks in the future with the battery uninstalled in order to provide a smaller weight in the product description. Always read the small print and check to see if the battery is included in the netbook's overall weight.

Screen Size

Screen size can be a deal breaker for many potential netbook buyers. Some people just cannot adjust to the small size. Even though the screen's resolution can be increased or decreased, shrinking or growing the size of icons and text, the overall physical measurements of the screen will not change. If you buy a netbook, you cannot upgrade the screen size, so make certain you purchase a netbook with a screen size you can work with.

Figure 1-4 shows the measurements of my netbook's screen. Netbooks with larger and smaller screens exist, and I chose one of the larger screen sizes available: 10.2 inches.

One thing to consider when looking at various screen sizes is the resolution of the display. Icons and text displayed on these screens is small—really small. Some readers might find it extremely difficult to read these displays. And even though my netbook's most basic resolution is 800x600, changing to this resolution really doesn't give me much improvement.

As with every feature of a netbook, this is one for you to check with your own eyes to determine whether you can work with the screen size and resolution provided. Buying a netbook online is one of the best ways to save money, but unless you've been able to view a potential model in person, it can make the purchase a bit like flying blind. If giving a netbook a field test is out of the question, find out as much information as you can about the screen resolution and other factors (such as keyboard size, discussed next). Get exact measurements if you can! Then compare these numbers with netbooks you can actually pick up and try in person.

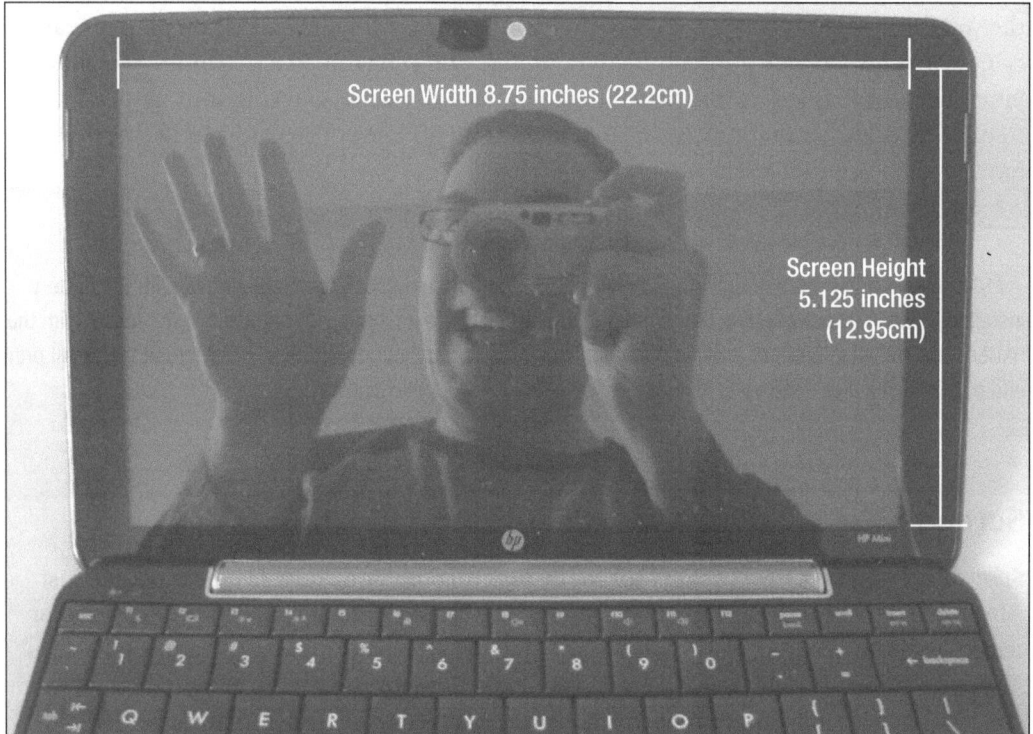

Figure 1-4. *My netbook's screen size is on the larger end of available sizes.*

Keyboard Size

Believe it or not, the small keyboard size is often the primary reason someone chooses not to purchase a netbook. Netbook keyboards typically come in two sizes—Standard and Frustrating. Let me explain.

Let's consider a standard keyboard that you might use with a desktop computer. That standard keyboard is sized just right for most fingers. When you press the A key, you get an A and not the neighboring S because your pinky accidentally got too close to the S key. Laptops also typically provide a standard-sized keyboard. The ugly truth is that I cannot blame these standard keyboards for my typing errors due to the keys being too small. Fortunately for me, my netbook has keys that are the same size as those found on my laptop; my typing speed hasn't suffered.

I can't provide actual numbers to you here because, frankly, even full-size keyboard key sizes fluctuate a bit. In my opinion, full-size keys seem to typically be about one-half inch square in size. Even if they're a little tapered at the top, the surface area is still large enough for your fingertips to rest solidly on top without touching the neighboring keys.

But that's not the case with some of the keyboards you'll find on many netbooks. Figure 1-5 shows a comparison of my netbook's keys to a full-size keyboard.

Figure 1-5. *Keyboards come in a variety of sizes, so it's important to try out the keyboard on a netbook before making a purchase, if at all possible.*

My netbook's keys are squeezed tightly into the case, stretching from the far left to the far right, but they manage to provide a large enough surface area to prevent typing errors. Not all netbook keyboards can say that, so I'm forced to repeat myself here—always try to test a netbook that you're considering for purchase.

Touchpad

A touchpad seems to be standard equipment for most netbooks sold today. This is no surprise given that the purpose of the netbook is to be small and portable; requiring an external mouse means having to carry another item with your netbook. I actually have a small USB mouse that I carry in my netbook bag for those times when a mouse is more comfortable, and I have the space to use it.

Although touchpads are fairly easy to use, you need to be aware that the touchpad buttons come in two different layouts. Figure 1-5 shows my netbook's touchpad—notice that the left button and right button are to the left and right of the touchpad, respectively. Some netbooks place the buttons below the touchpad (which is a standard layout for larger laptops). Many netbook users dislike the placement of the buttons on my netbook—the fact that I'm fine with my netbook's button placement and others aren't illustrates the importance of trying out any netbook in person before you put your money down.

Figure 1-6. *Netbook touchpads often come with the buttons placed on the left and right sides.*

■ Note I have yet to see any netbook that uses the embedded small pointer found in the center of the keyboard. You place your fingertip on the pointer, apply pressure, and move your finger to move the mouse pointer on screen. You might find a netbook available that has this option, and it's definitely worth trying out if you dislike touchpads.

Web Cam

Not all netbooks come with built-in web cams, but it's a nice feature. If you use Skype or a similar service (www.skype.com) and like to use VoIP (Voice over IP)—basically using your Internet connection to make free phone calls—the built-in web cam allows the person on the other end of the call to see you. I'll cover Skype in Appendix C.

If you want the web cam feature, but it doesn't come with a netbook you like, don't worry: cheap web cams can be purchased for less than $50.00 that plug directly into a USB port. You typically clip the external web cam to the top of the netbook's lid where it's less likely to get knocked off the table.

You can see my netbook's built-in web cam in Figure 1-7; it sits top-center above the LCD screen's surface and doesn't interfere with my screen viewing.

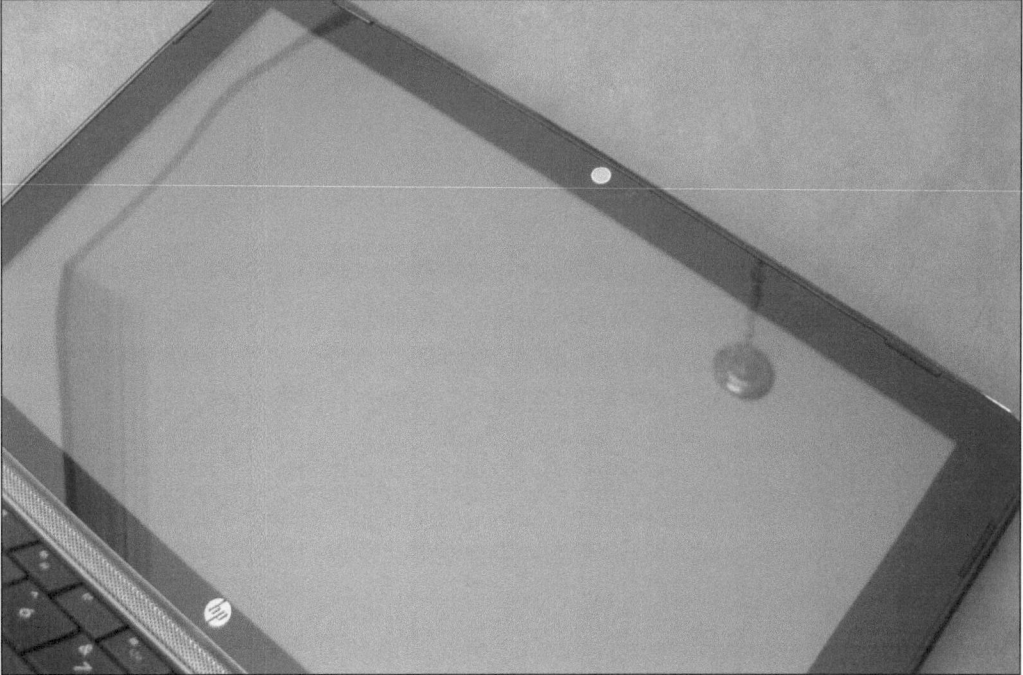

Figure 1-7. *You can find a built-in web cam on many netbook models.*

If you decide to purchase an external web cam for your netbook, make sure you verify that the camera is compatible with your netbook's operating system. Most web cams come with a CD/DVD that contains the software required for Windows to recognize the device. If you are running a newer version of Windows (such as Windows 7) and find that the web cam isn't compatible with your operating system, take a visit to the web cam's web site and see if that company has released a software update for the camera; it's a safe bet the company will have an update available that you can download for free.

Speakers

No netbook is going to win an award for outstanding sound. Sound requires power, and your netbook has been designed to minimize power consumption. Because of this, you can expect most netbooks to generate a lesser sound volume than what you find in laptops and desktop computers.

You might find your netbook's speakers on the sides, bottom, front, or top. Space is limited, of course, so manufacturers get creative when placing them. Figure 1-8 shows how my speakers are embedded in the hinge used to open and close the netbook's lid.

Figure 1-8. *Speakers are often located in odd locations on a netbook, such as the hinge.*

If you absolutely require better sound than your netbook can produce, you can always purchase an external sound card or peripheral that receives power from a wall adapter and allows for external speakers to be plugged in. Speakers that plug into a USB port are another option, but again, because they're receiving their power via USB, they're not likely to have the best sound.

Network Adapter Port

Most netbooks come with a built-in Wireless Internet Adapter (see the next section for more details). This means that if your home, office, or coffee shop provides WiFi Internet access, you can use the built-in wireless adapter to hop on the Internet.

I said most netbooks because a small number do not come with built-in wireless support. Those that do not will typically have a built-in Ethernet adapter port like the one shown in Figure 1-9. These are identical to the ones you'll find in desktops and many laptops and accept what is called an Ethernet cable—it's similar to a phone cable but with a little bit bigger plug on the end.

Figure 1-9. *An Ethernet port can often be found on the side of a netbook.*

You might be fortunate enough to find a netbook that has both adapters: wireless and Ethernet. Current wireless adapters operate at speeds around 54Mbps (megabits per second), while Ethernet adapters typically operate at 100Mbps—potentially twice as fast. Most of the time, you should find wireless fine for accessing the Internet, checking email, and even watching streaming videos. But if you happen to be in a location that doesn't support wireless or has a nearby and available Ethernet connection, you might just want to connect using your Ethernet adapter for the best speeds possible with your netbook.

The bottom line: Netbooks are designed for portability and, with the increasing popularity and growth of wireless Internet access across the globe, there's no reason to purchase a netbook that doesn't have a built-in wireless adapter. The best choice is a netbook that has both wireless and Ethernet adapters built-in, but ultimately your choice should be made based on where and how you expect to use your netbook.

USB

All netbooks come with at least one USB port, as seen in Figure 1-10. Two is better. And don't worry about the different versions of USB; these days, netbooks come with USB 2.0 (versus the earlier, slower 1.1 version).

Figure 1-10. *USB ports are a must-have feature for netbooks.*

If you find a netbook with no USB ports, you should seriously consider looking elsewhere. Because netbooks do not come with built-in CD/DVD drives, netbook users must find alternate methods of backing up files, installing software, and completing other tasks. (See Chapter 2 for more on the various hardware options you might consider purchasing as a netbook owner.)

Almost every type of peripheral device you buy these days—whether it's a printer, scanner, camera, mouse, or whatever—can be found in a USB version. I'll talk more in Chapter 2 about USB, but for now, you need to keep in mind that USB is the primary method for expanding the usefulness of your netbook. When comparing netbooks, rank USB ports high on your list of required hardware. (And keep in mind that you can "daisy chain" USB hubs, plugging one hub into another hub, thereby creating the "chain" and increasing the number of available USB ports.)

Color

Yes, color is a big deal for many people. In the late 1990s, the reign of the beige desktop computer ended and computer manufacturers began offering computers in a variety of colors. Why should netbooks be any different? White, black, or silver are the most common colors you'll find out there, but you're going to start seeing more color options as more companies begin to offer their own netbooks. Also, don't be surprised if some netbook manufacturers begin to offer customers the ability to customize the netbook's lid with graphics!

It's a bit hard to tell from Figure 1-2, but the lid of my netbook is black with a small repeating graphic pattern. It wasn't a deal breaker for me whether the netbook was black, white, or silver, but I have to admit that the black goes well with my office. (My technical editor is partial to pink, and wouldn't buy a netbook in any other color.)

Don't make color your highest priority—compare netbooks and push color down the list. If you find everything you need in a netbook, and it just so happens to be available in your favorite color, consider yourself lucky and enjoy.

Miscellaneous Ports

In addition to all the hardware and external features of a netbook that I've described so far, you might find netbooks with some additional ports or features that I haven't described. I can't predict everything that netbook manufacturers might decide to throw into their netbooks, but I do know that one of the more popular proprietary ports that I'm seeing in many netbooks is a plug that allows you to connect a docking station. A docking station is a device that you snap your netbook into that allows you to connect other devices, such as an external keyboard, mouse, microphone and headphone jacks, memory card slots, monitor, and much more. Think of it as surrounding your netbook with a shell that "upgrades" it into a desktop PC.

Netbooks on the Inside

Now that we've covered all the things you might find on the outside of the netbook, let's look at some of the really important stuff on the inside. Fortunately, most of the items contained inside a netbook are fairly standard; it's hard for netbook manufacturers to get too creative with what they pack inside when you've got such a small container. The previous section covered items such as screen size, keyboard size, and color—these are features that have a wide range of available options and can help a potential netbook buyer narrow down their choices. The items in this section, however, are fairly consistent from netbook to netbook. Why? One reason is that netbooks are still in their infancy; manufacturers are just starting to allocate funds for researching new netbook hardware. The variety of hardware currently available in sizes small enough to fit inside a netbook shell wouldn't make for a long list. The same goes for power consumption, where options are limited because manufacturers must limit the amount of power a device pulls from the built-in battery.

But give things a year or more, and you'll start seeing a wider variety of options for netbooks than I'll cover in this chapter. For now, there are four basic pieces of hardware you'll find in netbooks: a processor, a hard drive, memory, and a wireless network adapter (WNA). For some of the options, you may be limited to no more than one or two choices. This will make your job easier when researching a purchase, but it will also give you an idea of the potential that netbooks have for explosive growth and development.

Processor

Today's laptops and desktop PCs allow for a wide range of processors. The two biggest names in processors today are Intel and AMD—but of the two, only Intel makes processors for netbooks at this time. (This can certainly change, and other processor manufacturers might soon begin to offer netbook processors of their own as the demand for these little machines continues to increase. For example, keep an eye out for the Texas Instruments OMAP3 chip, which uses extremely low amounts of power).

Figure 1-11. *The Intel Atom chip is a low-power processor in a small package.*

The current Intel processor found in over 90% of the netbooks available today is the Intel Atom, which you can see in Figure 1-11. (Believe it or not, that component measures only 15mm x 15mm.)

Netbooks are growing in popularity, but unfortunately the options available to you in terms of processors are extremely limited. As I write this, the Intel Atom is the *only* processor I'm finding in all of the netbooks available for purchase. But again, this can change at any time.

In the near future, you'll likely be able to select from a variety of power choices for the Intel Atom processor. You will be able to choose between different processor speeds and varying amounts of on-board memory (called caching). You'll likely be able to spend a little more and get a faster Atom processor or save some money by getting the low-end version. In the end, it will come down to a balance between price and functionality for the consumer. Consumers love to have choices, so expect processor manufacturers in the near future to start offering different versions of their netbook processors.

Hard Drive

When it comes to storing files on your netbook, you'll be using the built-in hard drive. Similar to the larger drives found in laptops and desktops, netbook hard drives come in a variety of sizes and types.

The two most popular types of hard drives that you'll find in netbooks today are the Hard Drive Disk type (HDD) and a new type called Solid State Drive (SSD).

The HDD uses platters inside a case; these platters spin as data is written to and read from them. The HDD is considered tried-and-true technology and is found in the majority of laptops and desktop PCs sold today. Storage capacities for netbook HDD devices run from 40GB (gigabytes) to 250GB, but this number is always increasing. Don't be surprised to find these hard drive capacities doubled or tripled every year.

As with desktop and laptop HDDs, these devices are sensitive to drops and power spikes. If you've ever had a hard drive die on you, you've most likely experienced this from an HDD device.

The SSD is a new type of drive that stores data similar to how it stores data on memory cards found in cameras and other digital devices. When the power is turned off to the device, the SSD doesn't lose stored data. While they're more rugged and slightly faster than their HDD counterparts, they do have drawbacks. Currently SSD devices are about ten times the cost of HDD devices for the same storage capacity. And the capacities available for netbooks are extremely limited mainly due to cost; most consumers purchase netbooks because of their low price. A netbook with a comparable amount of SSD storage space would be priced higher, defeating one of the main reasons for choosing a netbook. (My netbook, for example, has 60GB of hard drive space; this same netbook is available with only 16GB SSD storage for the same price.)

When it comes to making a netbook purchase, the standard rule for buying a desktop or laptop applies: buy as much as you can afford. You'll be amazed at how fast that hard drive fills up. There are options for gaining more hard drive space that I'll explain in Chapter 2, but you should buy a netbook with as much hard drive space as you can to delay running out of storage space as long as you can.

Memory

Memory, or RAM (Random Access Memory), does not refer to hard drive space. This is a completely different component inside your netbook. When you turn on your netbook and the Windows operating system (or other) boots up, parts of the operating system and applications that you choose to run (such as a word processor or web browser) will copy themselves from the hard drive to RAM. RAM communicates with the processor faster than the hard drive, so it's always ideal to have as much RAM memory as you can to keep the netbook from having to go and access the hard drive.

Netbooks typically come with 512MB (megabytes) to 2GB (gigabytes) of RAM installed. While it's possible to upgrade some netbooks with more memory, many netbooks will not support adding more memory than they come installed with. Be sure to check on the maximum amount of RAM that can be installed; RAM is cheap, so you might want to upgrade your netbook's memory later.

So, as with a hard drive, buy as much memory as you can afford. For me, I'd sacrifice and take a slower processor and lower capacity hard drive before I'd consider a low-RAM netbook. My netbook comes with 1GB of RAM (and is not upgradeable) and runs fast enough for me; however, I've used a similar netbook with 512MB of RAM (half of 1GB), and the speed difference was very noticeable: text scrolled slower, web sites didn't load as fast in my browser, and the built-in wireless camera was almost completely useless.

Tip Don't skimp on RAM. With today's hardware and the current versions of the Windows operating system, 1GB or 2GB is sufficient. If you find a netbook with more, give serious consideration to purchasing it because additional RAM will extend the useful life of your netbook.

Operating System

Netbooks currently support various versions of Linux and Windows. This book focuses on the Windows operating system, so your choices in this matter will be limited to Windows XP, Windows Vista, and the latest version, Windows 7.

Let me jump straight to the chase and tell you that Windows Vista is not designed for netbooks. It's too clunky, requiring significant amounts of processor power and RAM. Microsoft has addressed this issue by releasing a streamlined version of Windows 7, designed especially for low-power devices such as netbooks.

Currently, Windows XP is the version of Windows found on most netbooks, but you can expect Windows 7 to become the de facto standard for netbook operating systems.

Tip If you're worried about purchasing a netbook with Windows XP and not being able to upgrade it at a later time to Windows 7, don't worry. I'll explain in Appendix B what hardware you'll need to upgrade your netbook to Windows 7, as well as some tips on how to make the installation proceed smoothly.

One last item to consider when purchasing a Windows-based netbook is the Service Pack installed. Service packs are upgrades that Microsoft releases periodically to improve the operating system and fix bugs that are found. The most currently service pack available for Windows XP is Service Pack 3, or SP3. When buying a netbook that runs Windows XP, check to see if it includes SP3. If not, you'll be able to download and install it over the Internet, but it's large in size and can take some time.

If you have a choice between Windows XP or Windows 7, I highly encourage you to go with Windows 7. Support from Microsoft for Windows XP will stop eventually (possibly even in 2010) and running the latest version of Windows will allow you to take advantage of updates (service packs) that will be released. And new hardware that you might choose to purchase later may not come with support for Windows XP.

Wireless Network Adapter

Earlier in the chapter, I mentioned that many netbooks come with a built-in Ethernet Adapter. This allows you to connect your netbook to the Internet using a standard cable. But for many of us, the days of cords and cables are over. We want to be free of plugs and cables and anything else that tethers us to a desk or makes us sit next to walls that have power adapters.

Netbooks are all about portability, and most netbooks these days come standard with a built-in Wireless Network Adapter. It's not visible—it's hidden inside your netbook and doesn't require any cable. If you use your netbook to browse the Internet, download email, or engage in any other online activities, you have to have a wireless Internet provider. This might be something as simple as a wireless router in your home that makes your Internet connection available to any wireless devices, including your netbook. It could also be that "Free WiFi" that you see advertised at your favorite coffee shop. (And if you're still paying for WiFi access at your coffee shop, find a new hangout—free wireless today is often offered as an incentive by restaurants, coffee shops, and other places of business as a perk to customers.)

When shopping for a netbook, you might find all sorts of techno-babble when it comes to wireless technology. Here's what you need to look for: 802.11g. Not 802.11b or 802.11a. Look for 802.11g. That's the most popular form of wireless Internet technology found in computers today, as well as the version of WiFi most likely found in coffee shops around the world.

▆**Note** Wireless technology is still evolving, so always ask a salesperson or do some research to determine the current version of WiFi being sold and used in your area. For now, 802.11g remains the most popular iteration of WiFi.

What's Next

A netbook is a wonder all by itself. Email, Internet, word processing, and more can all be had with no additional purchase required. If you don't believe me, then jump ahead to Chapters 8 and Chapter 10, where I show you how to get free email and productivity tools (such as word processor and spreadsheet applications).

But if you want to know how to get more out of your netbook, you're going to enjoy Chapter 2. I'll introduce you to the numerous hardware options available that can make your netbook experience more enjoyable and more productive.

CHAPTER 2

■ ■ ■

Netbook Hardware Options

I enjoy using my netbook. I love the built-in WiFi. I love the fact that it weighs only two pounds. And I especially enjoy the looks of surprise from people who see me typing away at Atlanta Bread Company, my "second office." People are still shocked to see a computer so small that is actually useful.

Yes, I get a lot of work done on my netbook, but when I first purchased my netbook, I was always running into roadblocks. For example, my netbook has no CD/DVD device—I couldn't install software from a disc easily, and I certainly couldn't watch a DVD movie. The hard drive is only 60GB in size, so I had to be to be frugal when it came to downloading applications and games to install on my netbook. It has only two USB ports, and I was frequently using both by plugging in a USB mouse and my USB printer. I often connected my camera and video recorder (both USB) to my netbook to download my pictures and home videos, so I frequently found myself having to unplug the mouse or printer, swap back and forth between the camera and video recorder, and then reconnect my USB printer so I could print some of my downloaded files.

But that's enough complaining. I got a netbook to make my life easier, not harder. So I had to do some research and find some solutions to my problems. And this chapter is all about what I found, including some interesting solutions that you might also find useful if you're a netbook owner.

The title of the book is "Windows Netbooks on a Dime," so I'm a bit hesitant to go and tell you to spend more money. But a netbook is, by itself, a relatively inexpensive device compared to most desktop and laptop computers. You might consider that the money you've saved in purchasing a netbook could easily be applied to some "extras" that can make your netbook use more useful and enjoyable. So, as you read through this chapter, make yourself a Wish List—identify those things can make your (netbook) life easier and do a little comparison shopping to find the best price. When you have some extra cash in your pocket, make a purchase, and you'll probably find (as I did) that even small additions to your netbook can increase its usefulness tremendously. (And for those items I describe that are of no use to you, just file the information away because you never know when things might change.)

The Shopping List

In the sections that follow, I'll describe some relatively inexpensive hardware options that can help you increase the usefulness of your netbook. Although this list is by no means complete, I think you'll find one or more items that "you just can't live without." Some of these options include:

- a USB 2.0 hub

- a USB pen drive

- an external USB CD/DVD burner

- an external hard drive

- a USB-to-Ethernet adapter

- a USB mouse

- a USB keyboard

One last thing I should probably mention before providing more details about these items is that I rarely carry these items with me. I leave them in my home office and use them only when they're absolutely required. This allows me to continue to carry my netbook without a case bogged down with cables, external devices, and other items. These items are there when I need them, and they give me all the functionality provided by my larger laptop, minus the big, heavy, and loaded-down laptop bag (and minus, of course, the laptop's larger screen).

USB 2.0 Hub

This first device was a no-brainer for me. My netbook only has two USB ports (both version 2.0), but everything I have in my office is USB, including my mouse, extra keyboard, printer, camera, iPod, and my external hard drive (more on that shortly).

Figure 2-1 shows my USB 2.0 Hub. It's simple to use: you simply plug it into one of the USB ports, and it gives you three additional USB ports. (There are four USB ports on the stick available for devices, but the hub uses one of the netbook's USB ports, so you're only gaining three ports, not four.)

Some USB devices get their power from the USB cable, while others get power from a power cord. If you plug a device into the hub that requires no external power (such as a USB mouse), then the device works as if you plugged it into the netbook USB port. (Note that an item that draws power from the USB hub also drains the netbook's battery.) But if a device needs power from a power cord, you still need to plug that device into the wall because this type of hub doesn't provide enough juice to power those kinds of devices.

USB hubs come in all shapes, colors, and port quantities. You can find USB hubs that provide 4, 5, or even up to 16 extra USB ports. The one I purchased cost less than $10.00, is about half the size of a pack of playing cards, and weighs only a few ounces.

If your netbook comes with only one USB port, a hub is something you'll definitely want to purchase. If your netbook has two or more USB ports, consider purchasing a hub only after you've discovered whether you actually need it; when you find yourself swapping USB devices frequently, it's time to pick up a USB hub.

■**Caution** Most USB hubs sold today are the version 2.0 variety. But be sure to read the packaging and make certain your hub supports 2.0 devices. The older version, 1.1, is a slower technology and doesn't allow you to plug in 2.0 devices.

Figure 2-1. *A USB hub provides additional USB ports to your netbook.*

USB Pen Drive

I think I get a free USB pen drive every time I get my haircut. I'm joking, obviously, but many businesses give these away the way they used to give out pens and notepads with their company logo emblazoned on them.

Pen drives have replaced the old floppy disks as the modern way to physically transport files from one computer to another. Yes, you can always email a file or burn it to a CD or DVD disc, but sometimes you just want to carry a copy of a file with you, and pen drives are so easy to use. You simply plug it into the USB port, and Windows treats it as just another storage location.

Figure 2-2 shows a 4GB pen drive I purchased for less than $8.00 at a local computer store; the store also sold a 32GB pen drive for $60; however, I use an online file storage service (see Appendix C), so I went with the 4GB drive. (Can you believe that in 2004 this 4GB pen drive would have cost me more than $100.00?)

Figure 2-2. *A USB pen drive plugs into a USB port on my netbook.*

Some pen drives are sold empty, with nothing stored on them. Others come with small applications on them that let you do things like scan your computer for viruses or edit any photos that you copy over. At their core, USB pen drives are just memory chips stored in a hard plastic shell that let you store files on them. Many Internet Service Providers (ISPs) put a limit on the size of file attachments you send along with an email (usually anywhere from 2MB to 5MB), so a pen drive is a great way to copy that collection of high resolution photos (10MB each) from your friend's computer to your netbook.

Pen drives are also extremely useful for making an immediate backup of any critical files you might be working on. After I'm done writing this chapter on my netbook, I'll be making a copy of it on the pen drive I've added to my keychain. It's just extra insurance that I don't lose any of my hard work.

External USB CD/DVD Burner

If all you use your netbook for is browsing the Internet and email, then you're likely to never need to install any additional software (other than an antivirus program, of course; for more information on antivirus options (see Chapter 6). This means that the lack of a CD/DVD drive in your netbook is probably of no consequence to you and you sleep just fine.

But for those of us who purchase the occasional must-have application (cough... games... cough), we need a method to install that software. Most software still comes on those shiny little discs, so this means we need a CD/DVD drive.

Fortunately, netbook users who need a CD/DVD drive (or burner, which is a drive that lets you write data to a disc as well as read it) won't have to do without. USB versions exist like the one shown in Figure 2-3. This one is connected to my netbook and allows me to back up my hard drive, as well as install software. (It was $80.00 and, for me, worth every penny.)

Do you absolutely need a CD/DVD drive? No, because there are other ways to get information from a CD onto your netbook. For example, if you have other computers in your home (or office), you can "share" those devices and make them available over your home or office network.

■**Note** The steps involved in sharing a CD/DVD drive are different from operating system to operating system, so please consult your operating system's Help documentation for instructions on how to share its CD/DVD drive. (An easier solution would be to offer your neighbor's teenager $5.00—your expected wait time would be about 30 seconds, and you'd be in business.)

In some instances, you might also be able to copy the contents of a CD or DVD installation disc to a pen drive (see the previous section) and run the Setup.exe or similar installation file; this doesn't always work, but I've had more successes than failures using this method. (My technical editor also suggests using emulators that can run apps directly from the image file.)

Finally, you should know that the device in Figure 2-3 is a combination drive—it reads both CD and DVD discs and writes (burns) data to blank discs. It's actually getting more difficult to find a plain old external USB CD/DVD drive that doesn't have burning capabilities. Although DVD discs are slowly but surely replacing CDs, I would still recommend you buy a combo unit instead of just a DVD burner. DVD discs are still a little more expensive than CD discs, and sometimes you don't need to burn 4GBs of data (the typical DVD disc capacity); a CD disc can hold 650MB and that will often suffice. Save some money by purchasing a mixture of blank CD and DVD discs and use the DVD variety only when you need to backup more than 650MB of files.

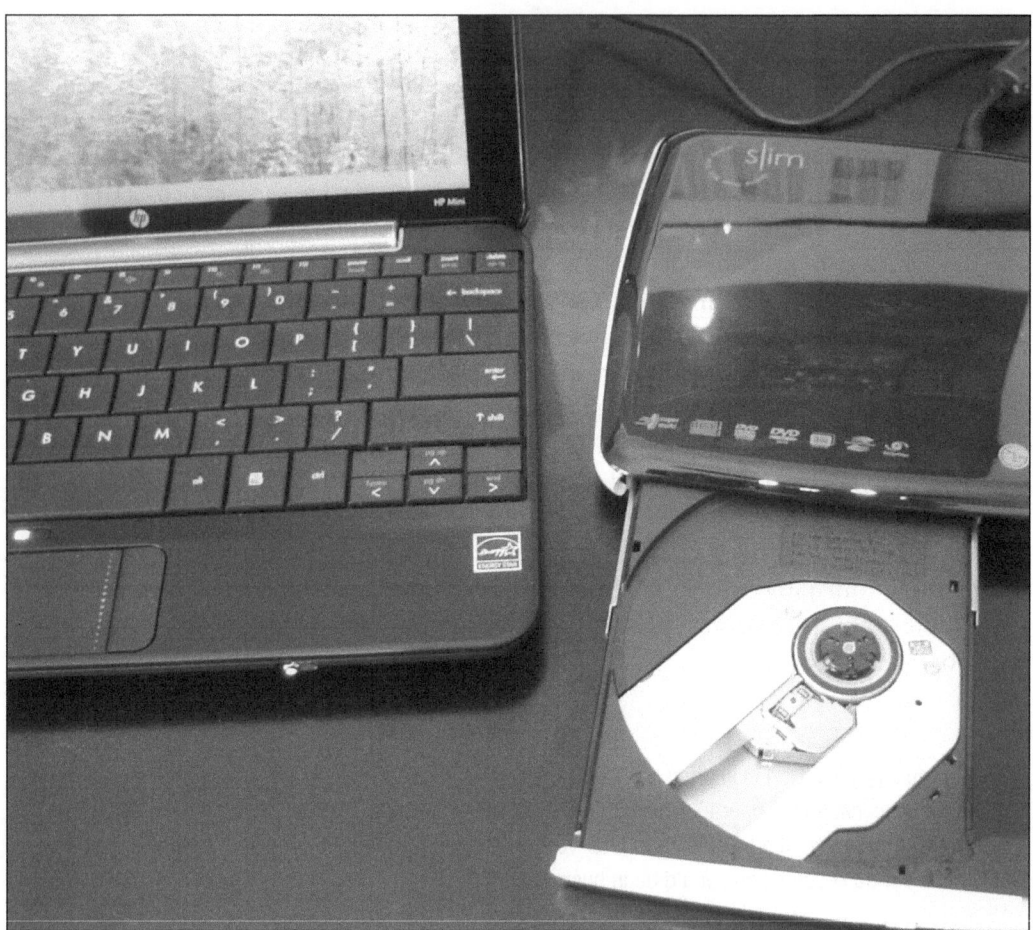

Figure 2-3. *I connect an external USB CD/DVD drive to my netbook.*

External Hard Drive

My netbook has a 60GB hard drive. It is running Windows XP Home and a small handful of applications (many of which you'll read about in later chapters). After right-clicking the My Computer icon and choosing Properties, I've discovered I have only 43GB of free space left.

43GB might sound like a lot of space, but it really isn't when you consider the types of files I store on my netbook. It's not uncommon for a word processing document with embedded photos (like the chapter I'm typing now) to approach 100MB in size. Ten of these chapters add up to 1GB. My books often have 20 or more chapters. And let's talk about my music: most of my mp3 files are only 3MB to 6MB in size, but I've got more than 2,000 songs that I like to have stored on my netbook (yes, I know I have a lot of music files; but they're all legal, and I've been collecting my music for over 25 years). That adds up to between 6GB and 12GB of files. I also have more than 1,000 photos (at about 1.8MB each)—that's almost 2GB of files.

Are you seeing a pattern? Do you have a similar problem? People like to have all of their files easily accessible, but the truth is that netbooks just don't have that much storage space (yet). This means you have to be picky about what you store on your netbook; everything else needs to be stored elsewhere. Fortunately, you're not limited to CD and DVD discs. These days, you can buy gigabytes of external storage cheaply, such as the one shown in Figure 2-4.

The great part about these external USB hard drives is that they're so easy and fast to use. You turn a USB hard drive on (it requires its own power via an AC Adapter that's typically included) and plug it into a free USB port. This makes the hard drive show up alongside your netbook's built-in hard drive (typically called the C: drive).

My USB hard drive shows up as D: when I plug it in. (I also have an E: drive that occasionally shows up when I plug in the CD/DVD burner I described in the previous section.) I can drag-and-drop files to and from this external drive. I can create folders and subfolders. I can even install applications to the D: drive! (Note that this requires that my external drive be plugged in and connected when I run an application installed on the D: drive.)

The cost of this type of device is more than most of the other hardware I'm writing about in this chapter, but keep in mind that an external drive can be used with any computer in your house or office that has a USB port. You can backup music, photos, and other files from any computer to this external hard drive—extra insurance should you ever lose your netbook to theft, fire, damage, or even through accidental deletion of files. (It's just good practice to always backup your netbook files regularly. If backing up to an external hard drive isn't feasible or logical to you, I'll also provide a short discussion in Appendix C on using online file backup services.)

Figure 2-4. *You can hook up an external hard drive that connects via USB.*

USB-to-Ethernet Adapter

As I mentioned in Chapter 1, most netbooks come with an Ethernet adapter built into the external case. Instead of using WiFi, you can plug in an Ethernet cable to connect to the Internet. Most, but not all.

If you frequently find yourself without a WiFi signal—in an office building, for example—and your netbook does not have a built-in Ethernet adapter, one simple solution that should work is to purchase a USB-to-Ethernet Adapter like the one shown in Figure 2-5.

It's easy to use this kind of device—simply plug the USB end into a free USB port on your netbook, then plug an Ethernet cable into the Ethernet plug on the opposite end of the adapter.

If you have high-speed Internet in your home, you probably have a DSL or Cable modem that was provided to you by your ISP. This device typically includes one or more Ethernet ports that provide Internet access to any computer that is plugged into a port. Plug the Ethernet cable that's connected to your USB-to-Ethernet adapter into a free port on your DSL or cable modem, and you should be surfing the Internet in no time at all.

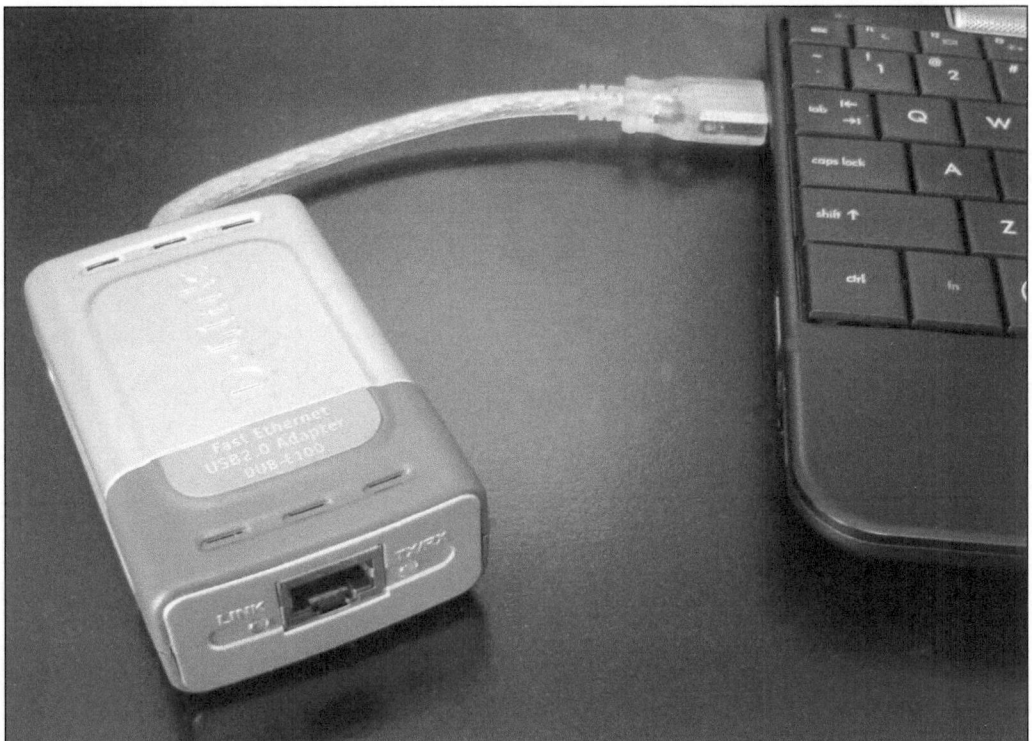

Figure 2-5. *A USB-to-Ethernet adapter can give your netbook Ethernet access even if it didn't come with that capability built-in.*

USB Mouse

Sometimes the touchpad on my netbook doesn't give me the ability to make extremely fine movements of the mouse pointer on the screen. For example, when I'm using a graphics program, using my finger on the touchpad doesn't allow me to get the mouse pointer at that exact point on screen where I need to place the corner of say, a rectangle. And games can be extremely difficult with the smaller touchpads found on most netbooks.

When I need a little more control of my mouse pointer (or, more likely, when I'm engaging an enemy player in my favorite shoot-'em-up game), I reach for the real deal: a mouse.

Figure 2-6 shows my USB mouse. It's relatively small compared to the mouse I use with my desktop computer, and the USB cable is short. Apart from that, it functions just like a standard mouse with two buttons and a scroll wheel on top.

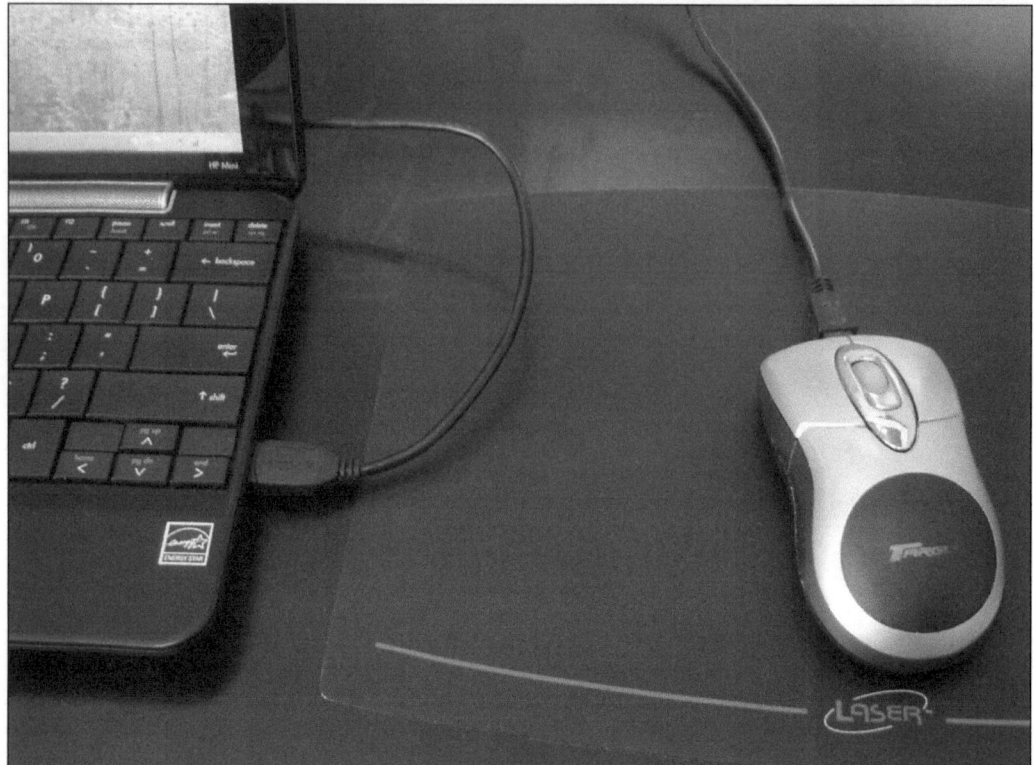

Figure 2-6. *A USB mouse plugged into my netbook*

This mouse cost me $11.00, but can you believe they had a cheaper one for $5.00? The only difference was that the cheaper USB mouse didn't have the scroll wheel on top. I use the scroll wheel on a mouse often, so it was worth the few extra dollars to me. The mouse is one of those devices that always seem to stop working after a year or so—it gets gunked up with dust and debris or just stops working one day out of spite. It doesn't matter! USB mice are so cheap that when that happens, I just buy another. (And next year, I'm betting that this exact same mouse will be even cheaper to purchase.)

I do recommend that you purchase a USB mouse if you ever find yourself using your netbook on a tabletop. It's a cheap and useful device that can make certain netbook tasks a little easier.

■**Tip** If you purchase an optical USB mouse, you might also want to purchase a cheap little mousepad that's designed for optical mice. Figure 2-6 shows my mousepad—it has a special bottom that sticks to the desk and won't move, but it can be pulled up easily when I'm done using it. It also features a lightly textured surface, which helps with the accuracy of the optical mouse.

USB Keyboard

If you look back to Figure 1-4, you can see that my netbook has a keyboard with fairly normal-sized keys. Because I type a lot, I need a netbook with keys big enough that I won't be using Backspace to correct all my spelling mistakes due to hitting the wrong key.

But not all netbooks come with the larger keys—many netbooks have keys that are the size of a No. 2 pencil's eraser. For purposes of email or typing up blog entries and entering your shipping information for an online purchase, small keys might not be a big issue. But if the netbook is your primary computer (or only computer), and you find yourself needing the services of a more standard keyboard, you're in luck.

Figure 2-7 shows a standard USB keyboard that can easily plug into one of your netbook's USB ports (or a USB hub).

Figure 2-7. *A USB keyboard*

One nice advantage of using a standard keyboard is the number pad on the right side of the device. My big ol' laptop (Boat Anchor) doesn't even have a number pad, and some applications are easier to use with a number pad (spreadsheets, for example). I've been teaching myself to use a free 3D-animation application called Blender (www.blender.org) and many of the shortcut keys used by this app are found on the number pad. For this reason, I'm seriously considering purchasing a small and portable USB keyboard for my netbook. (My desktop computer's keyboard, called a PS/2 is the type that has that round plug that is inserted in the back of the computer—this is no help at all unless I purchase a PS/2-to-USB converter, another expense that's really not necessary since USB keyboards were invented.)

I found a USB keyboard with number pad at my local computer store for less than $20.00, but I'm sure with a little more digging I could probably find one for less than $10.00. If you find that your netbook keys are just too small for long bouts of typing, you should definitely consider purchasing a USB keyboard at some point.

Useful Extras

There are some additional hardware items you might want to investigate that can add more functionality to your netbook or even possibly improve its performance.

If your netbook is anything like mine, the built-in speaker is puny, both in size and sound output. If you really want to crank up the volume a bit, you might want to consider purchasing a set of external speakers (with their own power supply). Speakers are available that plug into the headset port on your netbook or into your USB port. Make sure you purchase speakers with their own power supply, so you can turn up the volume as loud as you like.

This brings me to another suggested piece of hardware: the headset/microphone combo, as shown in Figure 2-8.

Figure 2-8. *A headset/microphone is a useful accessory for netbook users.*

It's considered rude at my local coffee shop to listen to music or watch videos without a pair of headphones. But I also like to use the Skype service (see Appendix C) to make free phone calls over the Internet (called Voice over IP or VoIP). To solve both problems, I purchased an inexpensive headset/microphone combo like the one shown in Figure 2-8. It has two jacks—one for the headset and one for the microphone—that plug into my netbook and give me sound and the ability to speak. (Many games also allow players to use the microphone to talk to other players—taunting and throwing insults is part of the fun of some games.)

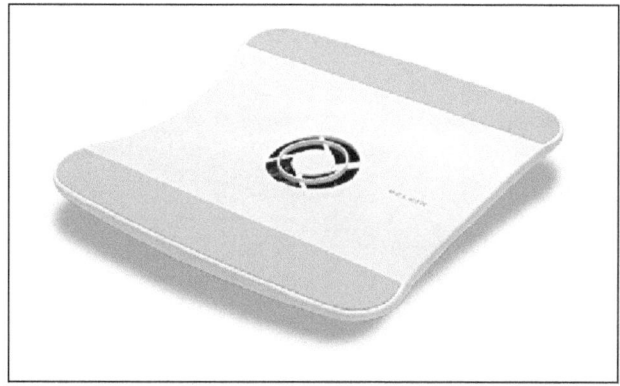

Figure 2-9. *A laptop cooler has fans that pull heat from your netbook.*

Finally, your netbook might be little, but it can generate some real heat—you might have noticed this if you've ever set your netbook on your lap for any period of time. A hot netbook isn't good for your lap, nor is it good for the hardware inside. To fight this problem, some users purchase an item called a "laptop cooler" like the one shown in Figure 2-9. You set your netbook on top and the fan (or fans) pulls heat from the netbook and dissipates it through the aluminum shell of the cooler. (The cooler gets its power via USB, which does mean your netbook battery will drain faster, but at least it won't burn your lap, right?)

What's Next

In this chapter, I told you about some of the extra hardware that you might consider purchasing to make your netbook more productive. In Chapter 3, I'll give you some advice on taking care of your netbook investment and giving it a longer life. Your netbook might be small, light, and easy to carry, but that's also a drawback if you forget to treat your device with care.

CHAPTER 3

■ ■ ■

Netbook Maintenance

I'm taking a big risk each time I go out with my netbook, and I should know better. A few years ago, I was carrying an old laptop down the stairs, and it jumped. You might argue that I dropped it, but to this day I still believe that laptop had a grudge and wanted to get me in trouble. It landed on the hinged edge and the LCD screen cracked in about four different places. I could turn it on and see most of the screen, but it was very difficult to work with and ultimately required about $200 in repair costs.

It could have been worse. Hard drives are sensitive devices and don't like drops and shakes. I could have lost a lot of personal files. Laptop motherboards aren't known for superhero endurance either and love to give off small wisps of smoke after being dropped. I've seen dropped laptops lose enough keys to spell out supercalifragilisticexpialidocious. Once I even saw a gentleman in the airport spill coffee on his laptop; he got so angry he threw the laptop in a nearby garbage can—true story. It wasn't a pretty sight.

Fortunately, I've learned (and seen) some hard lessons that you don't have to learn the hard way. This chapter explains all about how to protect your new investment. Your netbook isn't invulnerable, and it requires just as much care as its bigger cousin, the laptop, or its smaller cousin, the mobile phone. So, let's take a look at how you can keep your netbook safe, clean, and protected from some of life's ups and (in my case) downs.

Caring for Your Netbook

You wouldn't leave your car running and the doors unlocked while you were shopping, would you? And you probably aren't in the habit of leaving your mobile phone within easy reach of a toddler or a family dog. You recognize the value of these items, and you go to great lengths to protect and care for your personal items, especially those with a high dollar value. When it comes to your netbook, there are some easy and inexpensive solutions for giving it a longer, more useful life.

The Case

At the beginning of the chapter I told you I was putting my netbook at risk every time I walked out my front door with it. That's because I like to carry my netbook like a book, with no bag or other type of padded protection. Carrying my old laptop around in its bag was a real hassle, not to mention an additional nine pounds of weight.

I knew it would only be a matter of time before my netbook tried to make a break for freedom and jump, so I made the easy decision that I'd rather spend $30 on some form of padded protection than $300 on repair costs. Figure 3-1 shows my new netbook bag; it was designed specifically for portable devices, and it can hold a netbook up to 13 inches in length.

Figure 3-1. *My netbook will no longer be able to make risky jumps from my hands.*

There are two things I really like about this bag. First, it's made of some super-lightweight material that also repels liquids, such as those from my toddler's juice cup. Second, it has just enough pockets to hold a couple of items I discussed in Chapter 2: an external mouse and a pen drive. It holds my netbook and its power cord snugly inside the main compartment and, best of all, weighs only three pounds with the mouse and pen drive. (Oh, and it doesn't look like I'm carrying a purse. Double win!)

The Screen

If your netbook is like mine, you don't have a whole lot of LCD screen real estate. Netbook screens are small to begin with, so it's a good idea to keep the viewable area you do have be as clean as possible.

You might have seen special "screen wipes" available for sale at computer stores. They come in little packages of 10 or 15 wipes for $5. Are they serious?

In a pinch, you can use a soft cotton cloth lightly dipped in distilled water to remove smudges and fingerprints. Never use tap water—the minerals in the water can damage your screen and leave a white residue that won't appear right away. Also, be careful not to press hard on the screen surface, and be sure to wipe in only one direction; simply wipe and let the water do the work. Oh, and it's easier to see smudges when the netbook is turned off.

If you're as proud of your little netbook as I am of mine, give the screen an occasional cleaning—nothing is more embarrassing than having someone borrow your netbook to check email or sport scores and complain about the smears and smudges.

The Keyboard

Like its screen, a netbook's keyboard is a hotspot for dirt, dust, and debris. From cookie crumbs to eyelashes, keyboards always seem to collect all kinds of detritus.

One of the easiest ways to clean a keyboard is simply to turn it upside down (when the netbook is turned off) and give it a little gentle shaking. Don't shake it so violently that it can fly from your hands, though. This kind of shake will get rid of those larger bits and pieces that really can't get between or under the keys. (You can also purchase a little brush to get down into the nooks and crannies of the keys.)

For the smaller stuff, you should consider purchasing a single can of compressed air from your computer store (see Figure 3-2).

Don't turn the can sideways or upside down because the compressed air can quickly turn from gas to liquid. Instead, hold the can upright in one hand, and hold your netbook so the keyboard is vertical instead of horizontal. Hold down the trigger on the compressed air can and give the keyboard one or two quick passes. Do this weekly—a single can of compressed air can last more than a year if you don't go crazy trying to give your netbook the windblown look.

Figure 3-2. *A short blast of air can remove all kinds of debris from your netbook's keyboard.*

The Battery

You might, like many new netbook owners, find that the battery life of a netbook is often much longer than with the bigger laptops. Netbooks are small, and so are many of its internal components, and these components often demand less of the battery. This is especially true of the new low-power-consumption processors.

But there are still steps you can take to make certain your netbook's battery has a long and useful life. First, always try to run your netbook on battery power rather than using the AC adapter. Studies have shown that the batteries used in laptops and netbooks begin to deteriorate in performance when the user runs the device while plugged in.

Next, when the battery is drained, always try to recharge it completely, not partially. Many users will plug in their netbook for thirty minutes or an hour to get a "quick charge," but this isn't good for many types of netbook batteries.

I can already hear you saying "But I need to use my netbook more than two or three hours at a stretch, so I have to plug it in." The best solution is to purchase an extra battery for your netbook and swap a drained battery out for a charged one. Batteries aren't cheap, though, so be sure to shop around for the best price. Most netbooks come with what's called a three-cell battery. And, just as you'd imagine, a six-cell battery will have twice the battery life. A nine-cell battery would be even better! Do these exist? Yes, but unfortunately they're not available for every netbook right now, and many high-capacity batteries are available only for order from Europe (where netbooks are much more popular at the moment). Check out eBay (www.eBay.com) and do a search for your netbook model number. I found a six-cell battery for my HP Mini for $96—a bit pricey, but I might just grab one for an estimated five hours of battery life.

Caution Many of these high capacity batteries are larger in size than your original. When inserted, they will typically raise the rear of your netbook slightly, angling the keyboard towards you. This may or may not be an issue for you, but be sure to ask if this concerns you.

Over time, you can expect more battery resellers to provide high-capacity batteries for your netbook. Keep your eyes open at sites such as http://batteries.com or www.netbookmarket.com.au/ if you're in the market for a replacement or spare battery.

Serial Numbers and Installation Keys

You can keep your netbook clean and in a bulletproof Kevlar bag, but how would you identify your netbook if it were stolen? What if you were asked to prove you had purchased a legal copy of a piece of software? There are other ways you must protect your netbook investment besides keeping it physically safe.

Fortunately, there are easy answers to these questions. Do you have a digital camera? If not, go and purchase a cheap disposable camera. If so, I want you to do something right now—no excuses, okay?

Turn your netbook upside down and take a photo of its serial number. It's most likely on a small sticker, but it's possible the identification tag has been engraved on your netbook. Take a few shots in case you blur the photo.

You should also take a photo of the little sticker that Microsoft provides as proof that you're the legitimate owner of the version of Windows running on your netbook. Figure 3-3 shows my netbook's serial number and the Windows XP Home sticker. (If you ever need to use the reinstallation CD or DVD that came with your netbook, the installation key found on the Windows sticker is an absolute requirement for the reinstall to be successful.)

Figure 3-3. *You should photograph your netbook's serial number and Windows installation keys.*

Next, go and locate any software you've purchased recently for your netbook. What you're looking for are the installation keys (or codes); you've probably installed software where at some point during the installation it asks you to enter a string of letters or numbers, right? Well, those keys need to be photographed, too. They're usually found on a sticker on one of the CD or DVD sleeves that the discs come in, but sometimes they can be found on the software box or manual.

Obviously you can write all this information down instead of taking photos, but a digital photograph is easier to backup; you can burn a copy to a CD or DVD disc, save a copy to one or more computer hard drives, and even print out the photographs and store them in a fireproof safe or other location. Insurance companies also tend to ask for proof of "big ticket" items, so while you're at it, take all your software boxes, manuals, discs, and other hardware (refer back to Chapter 2) you can fit into a single photograph and take one final picture with your netbook right in the center.

■**Tip** One great way to save these kinds of "insurance" pictures is to use an online email service such as Google Mail (Gmail) and email them to yourself (see Chapter 8 for more information on using Gmail)! The photos are then stored in one or more emails that you can save or archive should something unfortunate happen to the original photos.

Theft Protection

In the previous section, I mentioned that theft is one risk that all netbook owners face if they take their netbooks out in public. I never leave my netbook sitting on a table, even if I can see the table from afar. It's just too small and easy to pick up and run with.

If theft is something you're seriously concerned about, and you're a homeowner, you should definitely call and get your netbook added to your list of property. This is one of those no-brainer steps that shouldn't cost you anything other than the time to call your insurance company.

Take advantage of the fact that you saved some money on your netbook and consider throwing some of those savings at a laptop-protection service. Some of these services are simply insurance programs that replace your netbook if it's stolen; others use technology to track and find your stolen netbook.

One of the more interesting is LoJack for Laptops—it uses software that's installed on your netbook (specifically, in the BIOS) and can help track its location when it is next turned on. LoJack states it recovers three out of four computers that use its service. You can check them out at www.lojackforlaptops.com.

CARING FOR YOUR NETBOOK'S INTERNALS

You've probably noticed that the security suggestions in this chapter apply to the physical well being of your netbook and not its operating system or software. For example, you might be curious about viruses or backing up your data. Don't worry—I'll cover all these subjects in more detail in the coming chapters.

For example, Chapter 6 introduces you to two 100% free antivirus applications that are perfect for your netbook—they have low system requirements for hard drive space and processing power that make them ideal solutions. And I'll cover backing up your data in Appendix C, including a short discussion that covers how to take a "snapshot" of your entire hard drive that you can use to restore your netbook in the case of a complete loss of your operating system, applications, and data.

What's Next

Your netbook most likely has limited hard-drive capacity. It's also designed for low-power consumption, so its processor probably isn't as powerful as the big laptops, and there is probably a limit to how much RAM you can install. All these factors mean you must take particular care when selecting the software to install and run on your netbook. Chapter 4 provides a brief discussion on how to find the software that is best suited for your netbook, including the differences between software installed on your netbook and software that is installed remotely, which you access over the Internet. The latter application type, which is referred to as Cloud Computing, is ideally suited for use by resource-constrained netbooks.

■■■

Netbook Software Options

Netbooks are still in their infancy; we're still limited to relatively small capacities when it comes to hard drives, RAM, and processor speeds. These limits mean that those of us who use netbooks must be vigilant about the type and size of the applications we install and use. These days, it's not uncommon to find popular applications with installation sizes of two gigabytes or more. And that's just the hard drive requirements; some of these applications also put a large demand on the processor and memory.

Keeping your costs down might (or might not) be the reason you purchased a netbook, but the reality is that you've purchased a computer for a reasonably low price. Why not try and continue this trend by locating software that's not only designed to run on a netbook, but also comes with an ideal price—free!

This chapter will introduce you to a few concepts you should keep in mind as you begin your search for software to install on your netbook. (Later chapters will focus on specific software titles and provides examples of their use.) You can find many applications out there that will place few demands on your netbook's hardware and even fewer demands on your bank account. Keep reading to learn how to find them.

Your Options

When it comes to obtaining software for your netbook, you have two options: pay or don't pay. I'm for the latter, but there are always exceptions. Let me explain.

Pay

The only advice I'm going to provide in this book when it comes to buying software is to always check the application's system requirements. Typically you can find these on the side or bottom of the software box (see Figure 4-1) or by visiting the company's web site and browsing for it there. If your netbook's hardware meets or exceeds the system requirements, then it's a safe bet that the software will run on your netbook.

Tip Companies frequently provide two different system requirement lists: minimum and recommended. The minimum system requirements listed will suffice, and the software will work, but it might run a bit sluggishly, and sometimes the user interface is not as eye-catching because the software tones down the graphics. The recommended system requirements is what the manufacturer feels is necessary to get the best results from its software, so try to aim for software where your computer system meets the recommended requirements.

Figure 4-1. *Software boxes typically list system requirements in very small print.*

You can purchase software at a retail store or online. You get a nice set of CDs or DVDs in a shiny, colorful box and, if you're lucky, a printed manual that explains how to install and use the software. (Unfortunately, the current trend is to omit printed manuals in favor of a PDF help file that installs with the software—obviously, the reason for abandoning printed manuals is to increase the profit margin of the company that makes the software.)

I have a few gripes with commercial software. Often, you can't return software once you open the box and/or install the software—even if it won't install properly, or it crashes your computer. Most stores print their specific return policies on the receipt as a way to prevent someone from installing the software and then returning it for a refund and continuing to use the software. Always find out a product's return policy, whether you purchase it at a store or online.

My second gripe has to do with upgrades. It seems that an increasing number of software companies are upgrading their software every year; you get an email or letter in the mail with an offer to upgrade your software to the current version at a reduced price. It might sound like a great deal, but it's often just a good money-making opportunity for the software company who provides you with a small quantity of visual changes or new features that really don't change the usefulness of the older version you're using.

So, before you go and spend your hard-earned money on that must-have application, let me ask you a question: have you done your research to determine whether there's a similar application available that meets your needs for less money or even at no cost?

Don't Pay

When I say you should avoid paying for software, I'm not talking about obtaining software illegally via download sites, copies from friends, or shoplifting. I'm talking about finding 100% free software that's available to you with no strings attached. Perform a Google search on "free software" and you're likely to get more results than you'll ever have time to investigate. Let me save you some time and frustration by giving you two better ideas when it comes to not paying for software.

The first is a concept called *open source*. Open source software is free software that's made available at no cost to you. (Okay, in some instances you might have to pay the shipping costs of getting a CD or DVD to you, but the software itself is still free.) The second option is called *cloud computing*. Most cloud computing software is free to use, but there are catches that I'll discuss shortly.

For both open source and cloud computing software, your netbook is the real winner in the end because these types of applications typically require less hard drive space (zero in some instances), less memory, and do not put as severe a load on your netbook's processor as traditional, locally installed software.

Open Source

What is open source? Definitions (and endless debates) abound, but the general consensus is that open source software is developed by an individual or group, that this software is available free of charge (albeit the user can be charged for shipping CDs and so on), and that it ships with its source code available for inspection, modification, and improvement.

Note Wikipedia has a great list of the 10 requirements set forth by the Open Source Initiative as that organization defines the term "open source." You can read the list by at this site: `http://en.wikipedia.org/wiki/Open_Source_Definition`.

While most open source software is given away for free (or with a small charge to cover shipping of a CD or DVD), some open source software comes at a price. This price is usually to cover the costs of providing tech support, printing a software manual, packaging the product, and funding improvements. However, even those companies that charge for their open source software are required to make the product available for free via download. This is part of the Open Source Movement's policy—you can modify the original source code all you like and then sell it (if someone will buy it), but if you used the original source code, you must offer the software at no charge in some format, typically as a free Internet download.

Individuals and groups who create open source software aren't usually doing so for financial gain alone. (Money can be made with open source software; for example, many open source developers charge consulting fees for training or installation, to name a couple ways of making a living—or at least some extra money—by being involved in open source development.) Instead, the developers typically follow the "software should be free" mindset and create software that they themselves would like to use. This open source software is often created to compete directly with Big Name Software Company selling Big Name Application. Open source developers, typically tired of paying high prices for software, dealing with buggy applications, and not having desirable features built into the software, instead choose to create a product that can compete (or try to compete) with the well-known commercial applications.

The best example of an open source product created to compete with a commercial application is OpenOffice.org (`www.openoffice.org`). OpenOffice.org (see Figure 4-2) has created a productivity suite called OpenOffice that contains word processor, spreadsheet, and presentation applications (among others) that compete directly with the applications included in the Microsoft Office suite.

Microsoft Office Home and Student (one of many versions of Office) typically costs around $150 for the basic collection of Word, Excel, and PowerPoint. At no charge, OpenOffice.org provides Writer (word processor), Calc (spreadsheet), and Impress (presentation). It would be misleading to say that these three applications offer every bell and whistle that Microsoft Office applications offer, but the OpenOffice developers are always working to improve their products, and regular updates add new features and bug fixes.

Speaking of features and bugs—that's one of the advantages of running open source software on a netbook. Many big name applications are often referred to as "bloatware." This slang term refers to the fact that these commercial applications are often large in size (gigabytes of hard drive space to install), come with more features than the typical consumer will ever find useful, and, worst of all, often have numerous errors (bugs) that pop up either because of sloppy development or rushing to get the product out the door. Open source applications, on the other hand, are typically less feature-packed and, because of the large number of developers who are reviewing one another's work on the applications, less likely to have large collections of bugs to crash your netbook. (This isn't to say all open source applications are perfect—rather, they are less likely to deserve the bloatware label.)

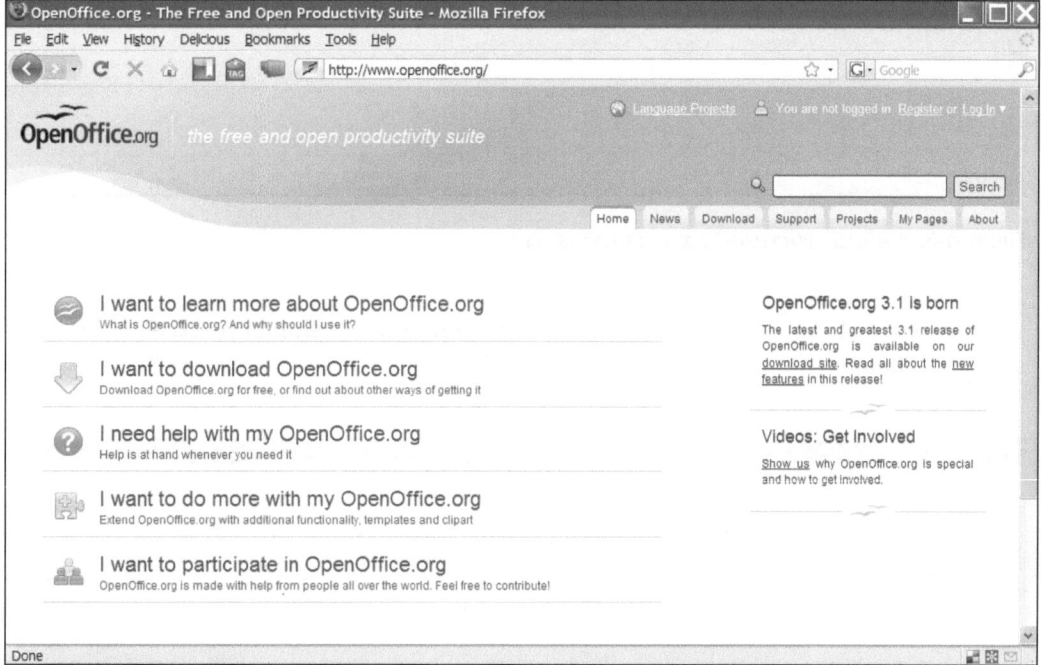

Figure 4-2. *OpenOffice.org provides its suite of applications free of charge.*

I'll be covering the OpenOffice.org suite of applications in more detail in Chapter 10. But to give you a hint of how these free applications compare to the commercial counterparts, take a look at Figure 4-3. This figure shows a blank spreadsheet in Microsoft Excel 2007. (Microsoft Excel is about $200 if you purchase it individually.)

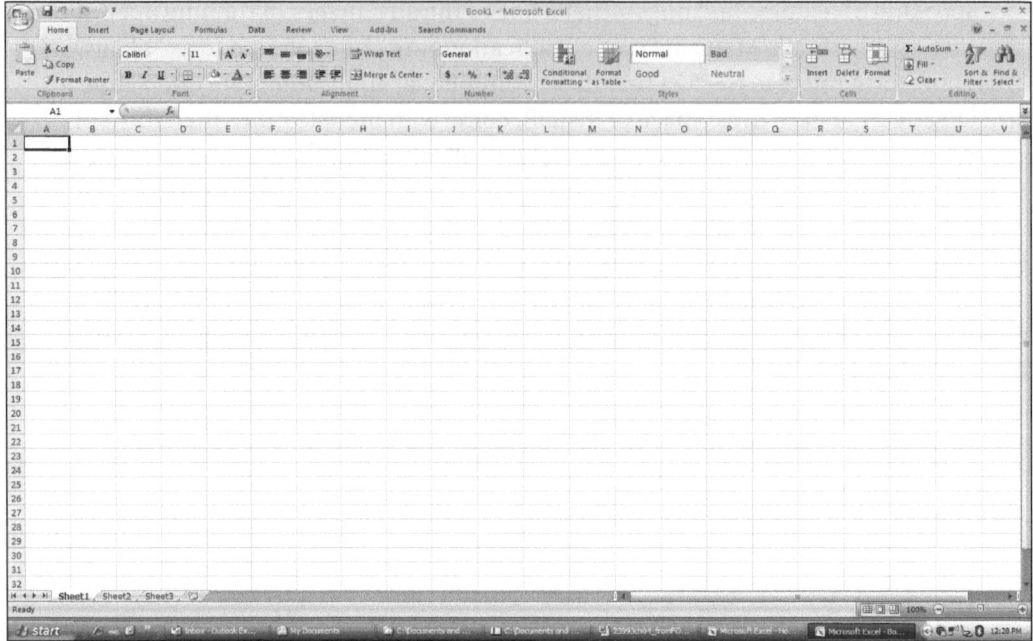

Figure 4-3. *A blank Microsoft Excel spreadsheet*

Figure 4-4 shows a blank Calc spreadsheet open. It works similar to Excel, but is considerably cheaper.

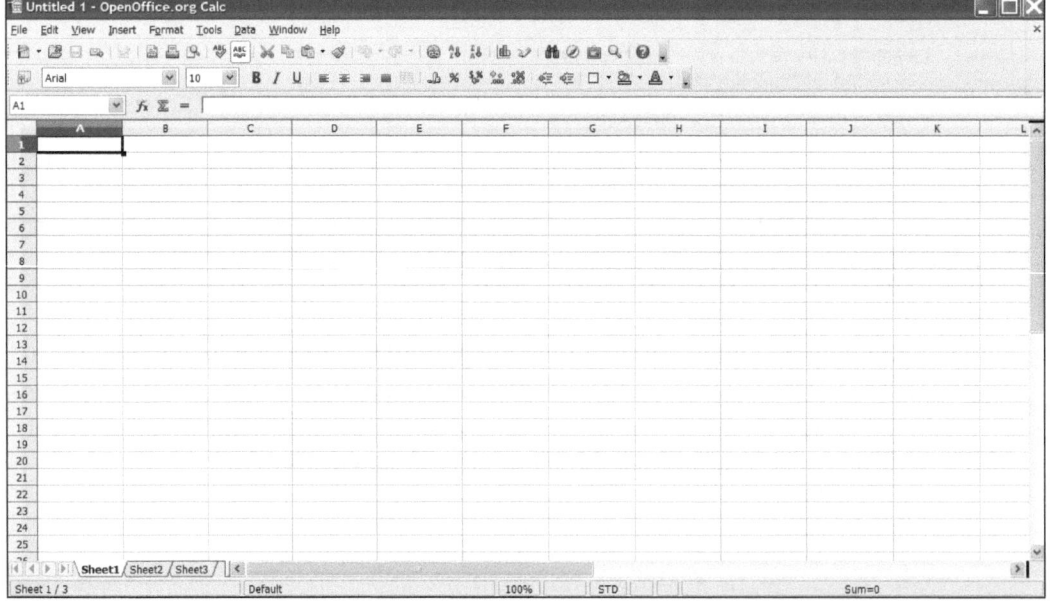

Figure 4-4. *A blank OpenOffice.org Calc spreadsheet*

As you can see in Figure 4-4, the Calc spreadsheet doesn't have as much "flash" as Excel, but consider this—Microsoft Office's system requirements show a minimum of two gigabytes (yes, gigabytes) of hard drive space, whereas OpenOffice requires 650 megabytes to install the complete OpenOffice.org suite (less than one-third of Office's). That flash takes up more hard drive space, but it also pushes the processor and RAM limits as well; you'll find your netbook running smoother and faster with OpenOffice's lower-demand applications.

As you consider the various applications you'll install on your netbook, always try to keep in mind your netbook's hardware limitations; open source applications are a great way to lower the demands on your hard drive, processor, and RAM. But there's an even better solution for those netbook owners who are looking for a way to keep their devices running fast with a minimum amount of installed software. It's called cloud computing.

Cloud Computing

I try to download and install open source applications on my netbook when I can. But recently I've been finding myself using a new type of application that requires nothing more than a web browser and an Internet connection. Let me explain.

You're probably familiar with web sites such as www.google.com—this web site offers (among other things) an Internet search service to you, via your web browser. You type in a word or phrase and Google performs a search for you, providing you with a list of possible web sites that might be useful. But take a look to the far right edge of the screen as shown in Figure 4-5. Notice anything unusual?

The Google search I performed on "CNC Machines" returned a list of sites and videos the search engine thinks I might find helpful. But along with the search results, Google also gives me a list of advertisements (both to the right and above my search results) that are paid for by companies hoping to get me to click their ad, visit their web site, and purchase something.

What I like about Google's solution is that the advertisements are not annoying (at least to me). They're obvious, but not glaringly obvious. This is the give-and-take relationship Google has with its users. Google offers us the ability to search for free in exchange for some online billboard space.

The Google search tool is the essence of cloud computing. You use your web browser to access a web site that offers up a service. The "cloud" is the Internet, of course, a name that derives from the way the Internet is commonly represented in process diagrams that illustrate how a computer accesses information over the Internet (see Figure 4-6).

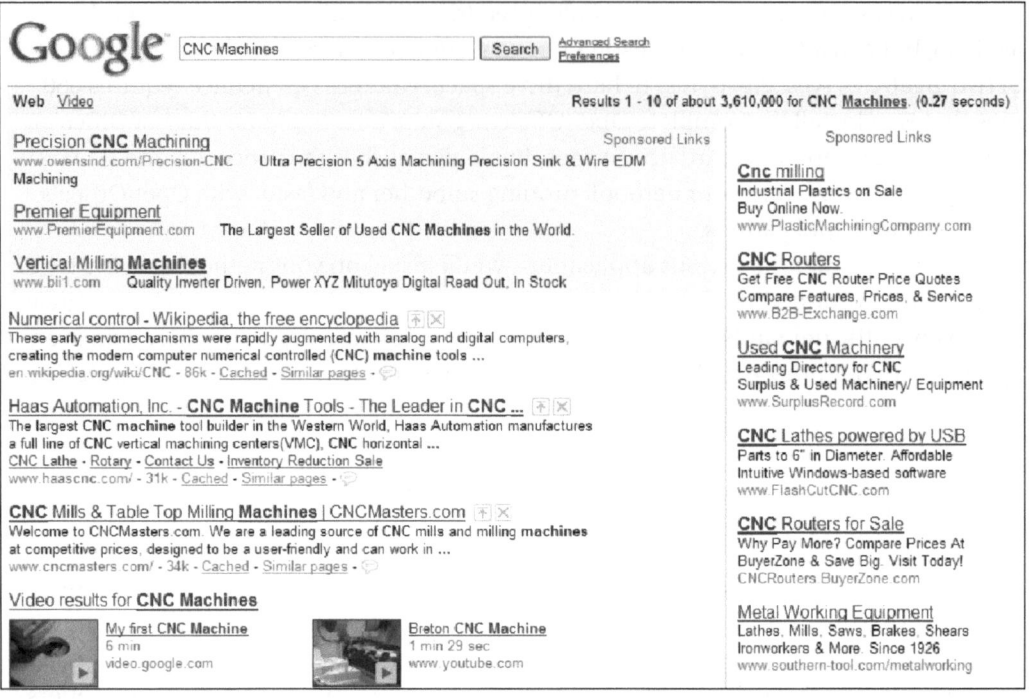

Figure 4-5. *Google has to pay its bills, and advertisements are its solution.*

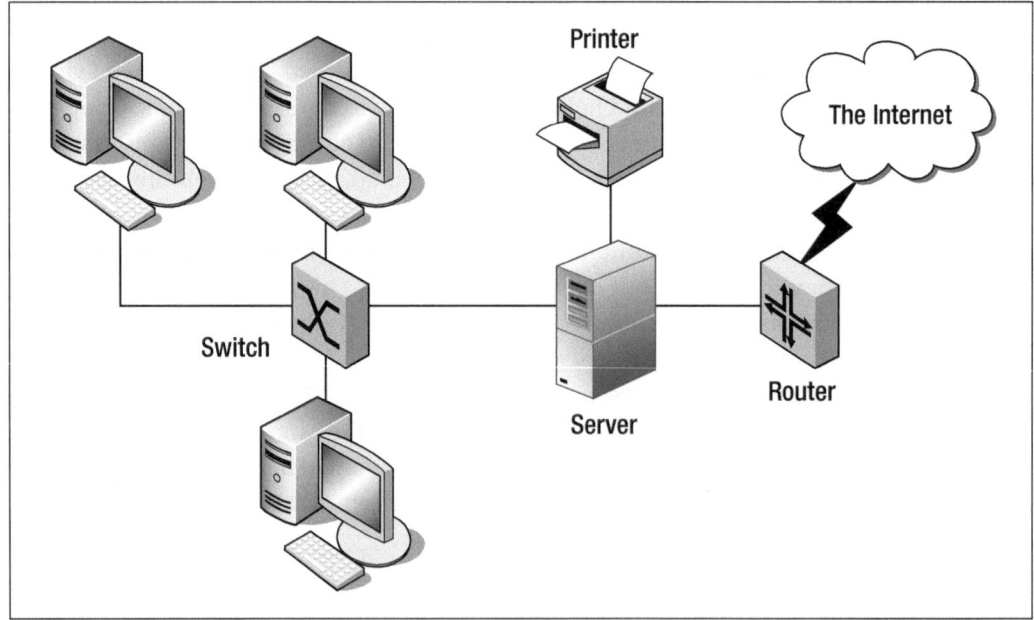

Figure 4-6. *Cloud computing gets its name from the generic cloud that represents the Internet. (Image courtesy of Wikipedia.)*

Online banking is another example of cloud computing. You visit your bank, log in with a username and password, and you're given access to your account balance and the ability to perform actions such as transferring funds and opening different types of accounts—all from your browser. More cloud computing examples include online newspapers (www.cnn.com), online email applications (www.hotmail.com), and even online games (www.casualcollective.com) where you can play games against the computer or other players—again, you access all of these applications from your web browser. (And let's not forget Amazon.com, where you can buy pretty much anything that can be sold these days.) All of these activities and many more can be accessed without installing any additional software on your netbook.

There are benefits to using online applications that go beyond not having to install applications on your netbook's hard drive. Take a look at Figure 4-7, which shows Google Mail (or Gmail), a free email service that Google provides.

Figure 4-7. *Gmail is a cloud computing email application.*

Gmail stores my email (and attachments) on the Google servers. This means that no matter which computer I use—mine, my neighbors, yours, or even an Internet kiosk at the library—as long as it has Internet access, I can login and check my email. I cover Gmail in more detail in Chapter 8, so feel free to jump ahead if you want to learn about it and start using it immediately.

Cloud computing is growing in popularity. Because you're using a web browser, all that's required of you is to remember the web address (URL) and your username and password, if necessary. A cloud computing application runs inside the web browser and handles things like data encryption and security behind the scenes. For those of you who are concerned about security, always look in the lower-right corner of your web browser for an icon like the one shown in Figure 4-8. The little lock icon lets you know that the web site is secure. (Note that the "s" in "https://" in a web address box also indicates that the Web site you're at is secure.)

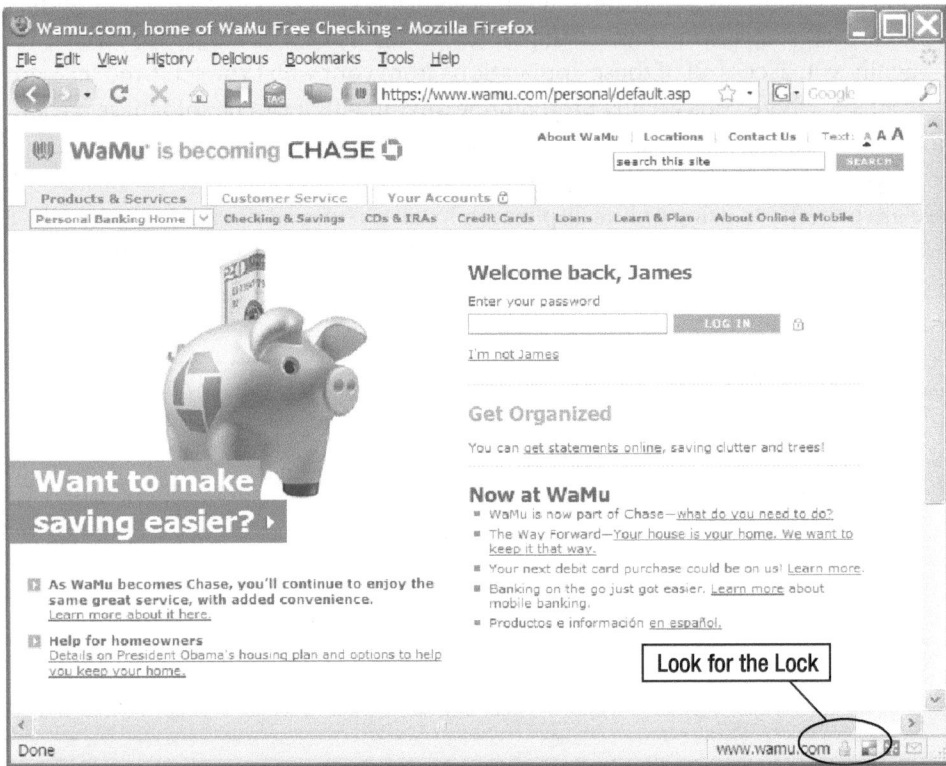

Figure 4-8. *Cloud computing provides security, but you should always double-check that the site you're visiting is secure.*

One last thing about cloud computing that you should know—many technology "experts" believe that cloud computing is not only going to become more prevalent and popular with businesses, but that it's likely that many popular services and applications will develop into a commercial or subscription model. Your bank might already be charging you for online banking services, and many magazines such as Consumer Reports already charge for accessing information on their web sites. Nonetheless, you should look for more companies to start offering their applications over the Internet through a browser. Of course, cloud computing is also heavily dependent on your connection speed to the Internet—if you have an Internet provider that isn't giving you the best bandwidth possible, your "in the cloud" experience can be very unsatisfying.

Microsoft is currently testing an online version of Office that it says will be free to use, but you should expect additional features (and by additional, I mean any new or advanced upgrades Microsoft might add to the software at a later time) to come at a price. So what about all that software you've purchased and installed on your computers in the past? Those companies are likely to develop online versions as well, which means you'll have to investigate even further to determine which software option is best for you, whether it's open source, cloud computing, or commercial software.

What's Next

Now that I've introduced you to open source and cloud computing, it's time for you to see some examples for yourself. I'll cover a small handful of cloud computing applications in Chapter 5; in later chapters, I'll introduce you to an open source web browser that I prefer (over Internet Explorer), as well as to two of my favorite cloud computing applications that are 100% free to use.

CHAPTER 5

■ ■ ■

Netbook and Google Docs

In Chapter 4, I introduced you to the concepts of open source and cloud computing. Applications that fall under either of these categories can be extremely beneficial to a netbook user. Most netbooks do not come with the fastest processors or largest amounts of RAM or hard drive space, so open source software and cloud computing applications might be the perfect software for your netbook.

I'll be covering a mixture of open source and cloud computing applications in this book; I'll begin by introducing you to a small collection of cloud computing applications that can get you working immediately if you lack any productivity application on your netbook.

I think everyone these days has heard of Google and its powerful search features.

Because Google is so Internet-centric, it probably will come as no surprise to discover that the company is a huge supporter of cloud computing. I've lost count of exactly how many cloud computing applications Google has released, but it has released cloud applications for email, calendar/planner activities, web site creation, blogging, and many more. (For a complete list, visit `www.google.com/intl/en/options` and be prepared for a shock.)

You've got plenty of time to investigate all of Google's cloud computing services (and I cover a few more in Chapter 8 and Chapter 9), but I'm going to start you out with one of Google's best and most useful collection of cloud computing services: Google Docs, which includes a word processor, spreadsheet application, and a slideshow creator.

Note The goal of this chapter isn't to teach you how to use a word processor, spreadsheet, or slideshow application; there are entire books written on each of these types of applications. If you're looking for training on any of these applications, please visit `http://docs.google.com/support`, click the application you wish to learn about, and prepare to be amazed by the quantity of detailed information that is available.

Your Google Account

You need to create a Google Account before you can begin using Google Docs. (Feel free to skip to the next section if you already have a Google user account.) Open your web browser and visit http://docs.google.com. Figure 5-1 shows the Google Docs Welcome screen.

Figure 5-1. *Google Docs is free to use, but it requires you to sign up for a Google Account.*

Begin by clicking the Get Started button. On the "Create an Account" screen (see Figure 5-2), provide an email address, password (twice for verification), and your location. Type in the letters you see on the screen for the Word Verification, read through the Terms of Service, and then click the button that says, "I accept. Create my account." Check your email because Google will send you an email with a hyperlink inside; click that link to verify you created the new Google Account, and you're almost done.

After you verify your new account, browse once again to docs.google.com and provide your email address and password as shown in Figure 5-3. Place a check in the box labeled, "Remember me on this computer." Doing so will automatically log you into Google Docs (or any Google application for that matter) the next time you visit the application's site. Leave this box unchecked if you'd rather provide your login credentials every time for extra security.

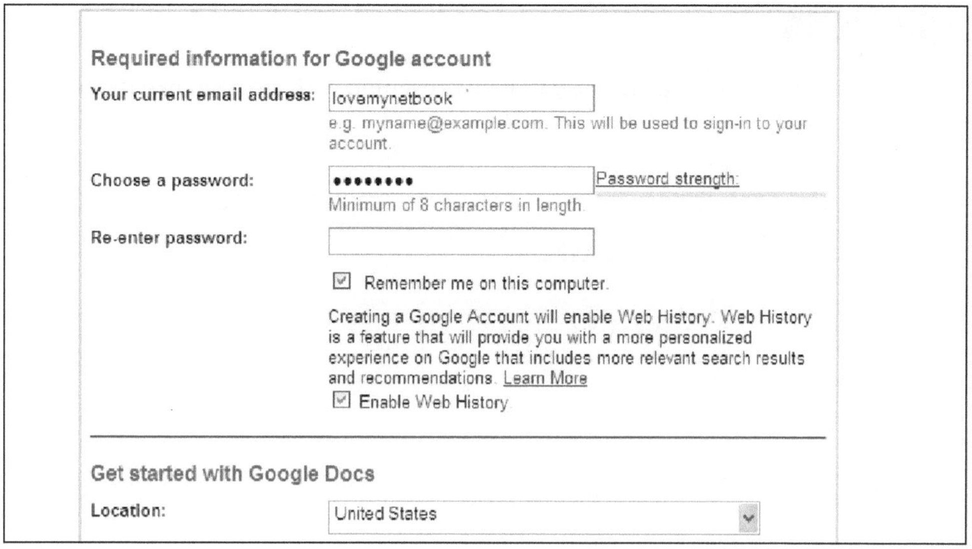

Required information for Google account

Your current email address: | lovemynetbook |
e.g. myname@example.com. This will be used to sign-in to your account.

Choose a password: | •••••••• | Password strength:
Minimum of 8 characters in length.

Re-enter password: | |

☑ Remember me on this computer.

Creating a Google Account will enable Web History. Web History is a feature that will provide you with a more personalized experience on Google that includes more relevant search results and recommendations. Learn More
☑ Enable Web History

Get started with Google Docs

Location: | United States ▾ |

Figure 5-2. *Create and verify your new Google Account before using Google Docs.*

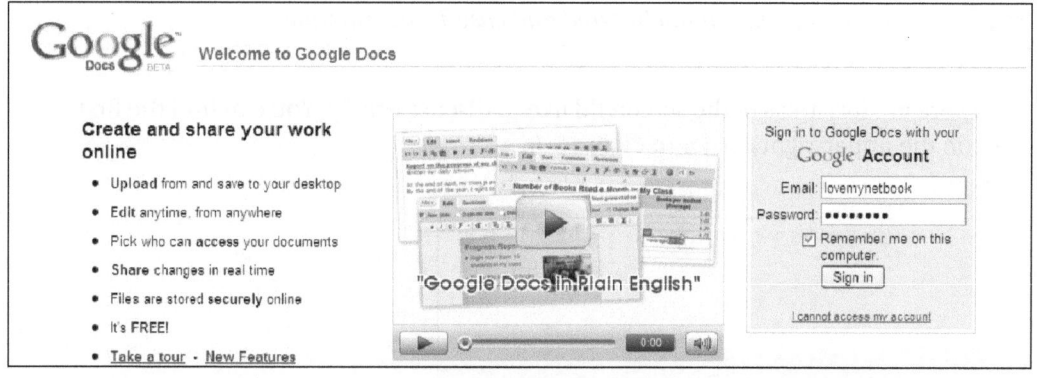

Figure 5-3. *Log in to Google Docs with your email and password to get started.*

Google Docs

The first time you log in to Google Docs, you'll be presented with a screen like the one shown in Figure 5-4.

Figure 5-4. *Google Docs has an uncluttered and easy-to-use interface.*

There are five areas of the screen I'd like to discuss briefly. You can find the first of these in the upper-right corner of Figure 5-5.

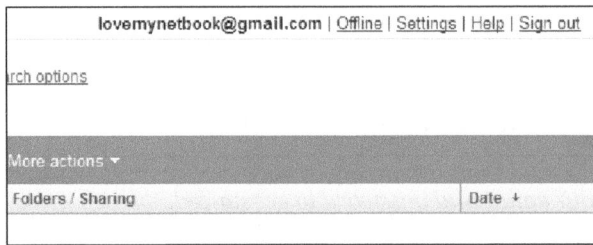

Figure 5-5. *Account options for Google Docs*

In the upper right corner, you'll always be able to see the email address for the Google Account you're using. I have more than one Google Account, which makes this feature useful. If you only have one account, this merely serves as a reminder of your email address. Other options include an Offline link that lets you use Google Docs even when you're not connected to the Internet. (Click it to learn more about how to use this feature.) I'll cover the Settings link in more detail a little later in the chapter, but for now all you need to know is that it lets you make some changes to how Google Docs looks and operates. The Help link is just what it says: it opens up Docs Help where you can type in questions, view video tutorials, and basically learn more about using Google Docs more efficiently.

Now take a look at the upper-left corner of Figure 5-6.

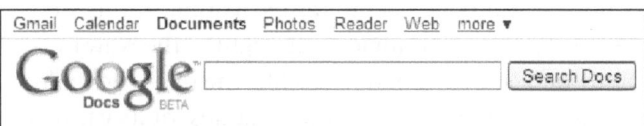

Figure 5-6. *Did I hear you say you want more Google cloud computing applications?*

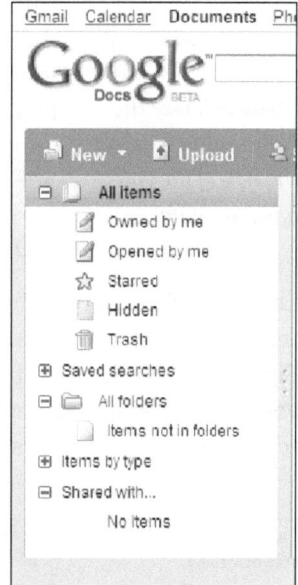

Google provides one-click links to its most popular cloud computing applications in the upper-left corner, including links to Google E-mail (Gmail, covered in Chapter 8), Calendar (see Chapter 9), and more (literally—click the "more" link to view them all). Feel free to click them now if you like; Google Docs will wait patiently for you to return.

Next, take a look at the left edge of the screen, as shown in Figure 5-7.

Figure 5-7 shows a Google Docs folder window. Clicking a folder (such as "Owned by me") displays any documents you create—text, spreadsheet, or slideshow—in the center area of the screen. You can click the Trash folder to see documents you've deleted, and you can also create your own

Figure 5-7. *Documents you create will be organized using the folders window.*

folders that are listed under the "All folders" section. You haven't created any documents yet, so this area might not make 100% sense yet, but I'll explain more about this area shortly.

Now take a look at Figure 5-8, which shows the Google Docs toolbars.

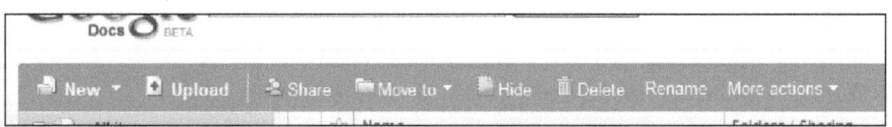

Figure 5-8. *Google Docs provides a simple toolbar that won't overwhelm you.*

The Google Docs toolbar consists of a handful of buttons and drop-down menus. You'll use these buttons and menus to create new files, rename and delete files, move files around to various folders, share files with friends and colleagues, and much more.

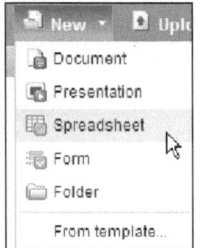

Most of these options are fairly self-explanatory, but I'll be covering these options in more depth at the end of the chapter, after you've learned to create your own documents, spreadsheets, and slide-shows.

Figure 5-9. *Use the New button to select the type of file you wish to create.*

Speaking of documents, let's go ahead and take a look at what Google Docs offers the netbook user in terms of applications. See that little downward pointing triangle to the right of the New button? Click it, and you'll see a list of options like the ones shown in Figure 5-9. (Google doesn't believe in cutesy names for its various applications, as you can see.)

Google Docs Document

Let's start by creating a simple word processing file. Click "Document" from the drop-down menu, and you'll see a new word-processing document open like the one shown in Figure 5-10. Notice that the document opens in a new browser window (or a new tab if you use a browser that supports the tab feature); you can click the Google Docs window to return to the Google Docs file management screen anytime you like.

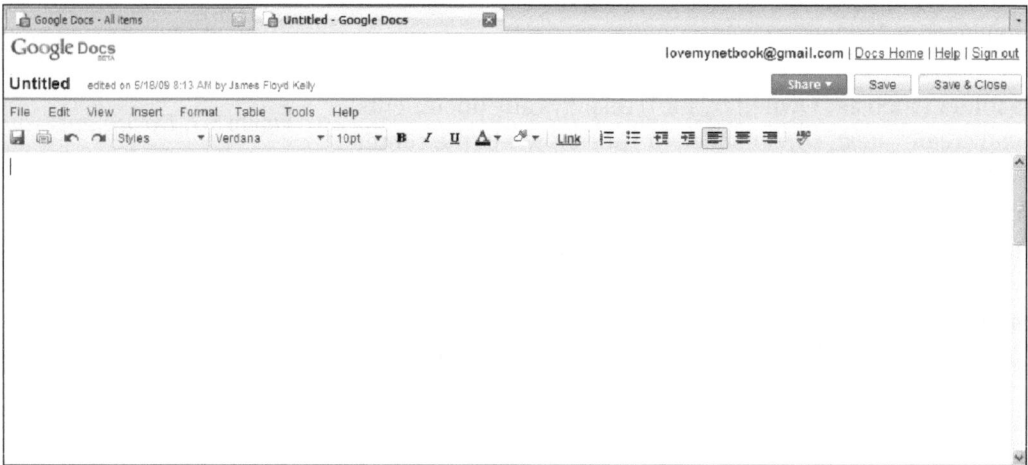

Figure 5-10. *A blank Document window opens, ready for you to begin typing.*

Document works like most basic word processor applications you're likely familiar with—you've got drop-down menus that include File, Edit, View, Insert, Format, Table, Tools, and Help, as seen in Figure 5-11. Most of the selections in these menus are easy to figure out, but I encourage you to click the Help menu and choose "Google Docs Help Center" if you have any questions on how to use a feature in Document.

The toolbar is beneath the menu bar, also shown in Figure 5-11. The toolbar contains buttons that let you change things like the font, font size, color of the font, and the text justification (left, centered, or right). Additional buttons let you save, print, and add formatting such as underline, bold, and italics. The Link button lets you add a hyperlink (URL) for a web site; when a reader clicks on the link, her web browser will take her to whatever web site you've specified. Finally, on the far right of the toolbar, you'll see a tool we all need sooner or later: Check Spelling.

Figure 5-11. *Document offers menus and a toolbar with familiar features.*

Before moving to Spreadsheet and Presentation applications, I'd like to show you another useful feature that's found in all three applications. It's called Sharing, and it's easy to use. I've created a sample document (see Figure 5-12) and, after clicking the Save button in the upper-right corner, I click the Share button. You can see the options available to me in Figure 5-12.

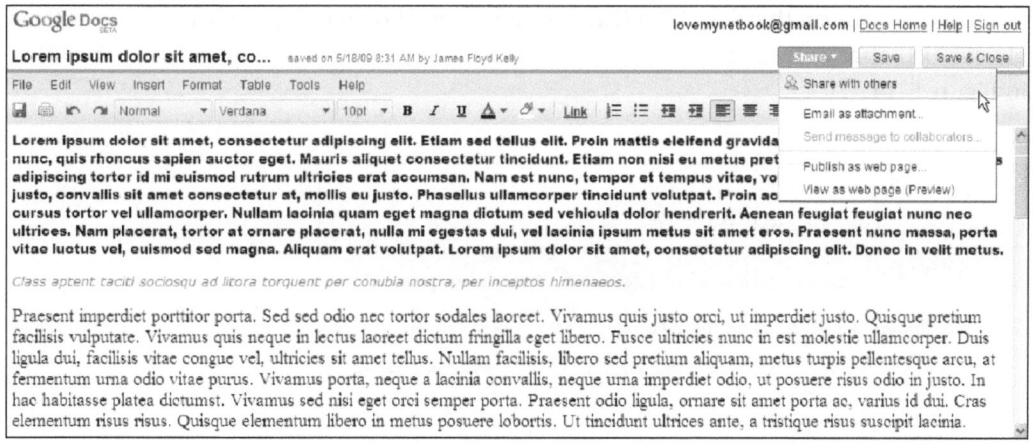

Figure 5-12. *Sharing a file is extremely simple with Google Docs.*

The two options I want to focus on here are "Share with others" and "Publish as web page." I'll start by clicking the "Publish as web page" option, which brings up a screen like the one shown in Figure 5-13.

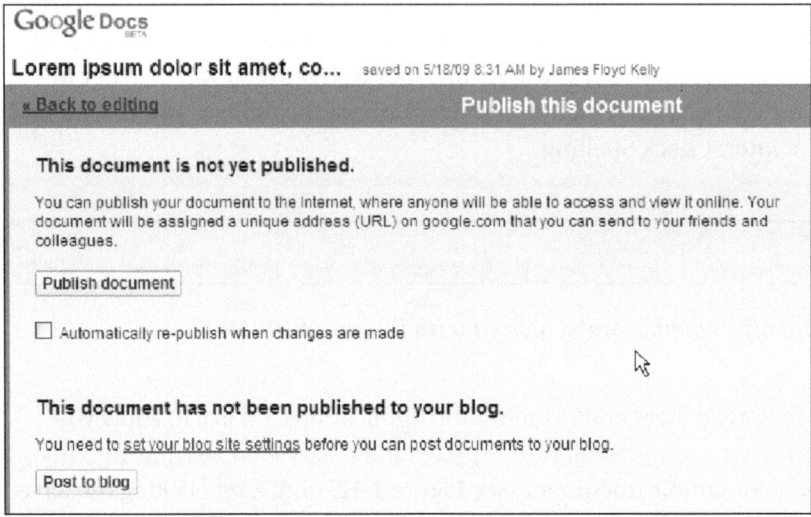

Figure 5-13. *You can choose to have your document visible on the Internet for all to see.*

Click the button that says "Publish document" as shown in Figure 5-13, and you'll be given a URL that you can email to friends, family, and co-workers. You can see this URL in Figure 5-14.

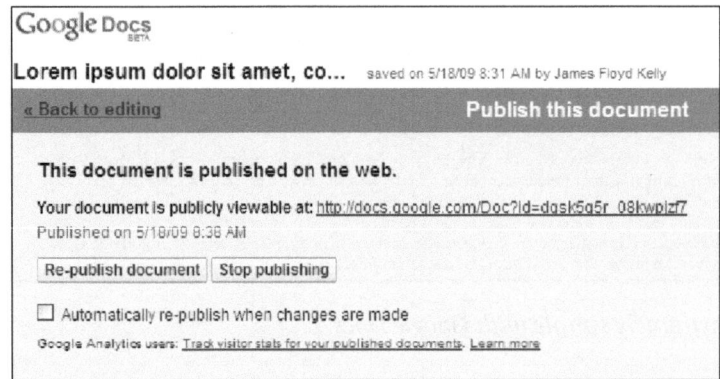

Figure 5-14. *Google will host your published document and provide a URL for viewing it.*

This document is being hosted by Google, so anyone in the world can view it (but only if they can find it). It's possible that your document might be what someone doing a Google search is looking for, so be aware that publishing it makes it available to others via the Google search tool. If you don't wish to let the entire world view your web page, you have another option: Sharing. Go ahead and click the "Stop publishing" option shown in Figure 5-14, and then click the Share button again and select the "Share with others" option, which brings up the screen shown in Figure 5-15.

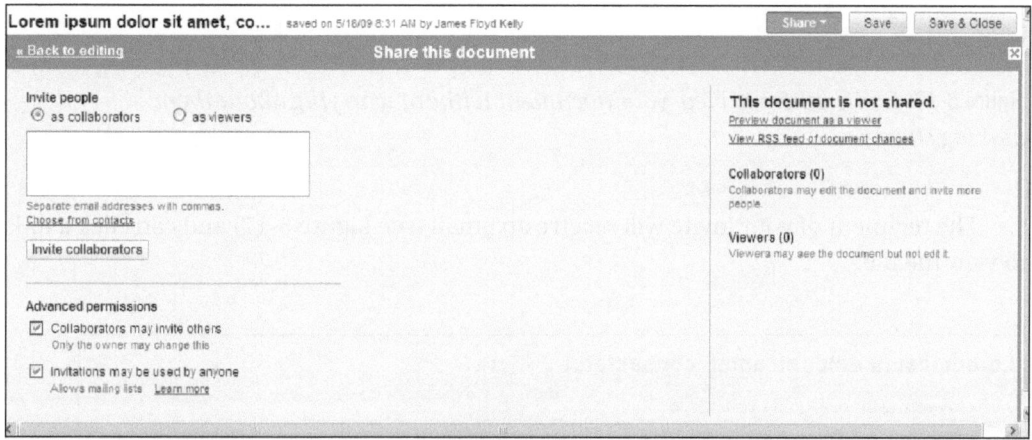

Figure 5-15. *Sharing your document allows you to limit who can view it or make changes.*

When you choose to share your document with someone, Google Docs requires that you specify whether that person is a collaborator or viewer. Viewers can only view the document; the ability to make changes is prohibited. Collaborators, on the other hand, are given the ability to make changes to the document, including deleting and adding content. Collaborators are even given the ability to invite other collaborators and viewers by default!

To add a viewer, click the "as viewers" option shown in Figure 5-16. Enter the email address of the person you wish to add as a viewer and click the Invite Viewers button. A new window opens that allows you to send a message to the viewer, informing him about the invite, as well as any details you wish to share about the document. Click the Send button, and your invite is on its way.

■**Note** Viewers and collaborators need to create their own Google accounts if they don't already have one. Logging in to Google Docs is a requirement for everyone who wants to view or edit your document.

Lorem ipsum dolor sit amet, co...   saved on 5/18/09 8:31 AM by James Floyd Kelly

« Back to editing   **Share this document**

Invite people
○ as collaborators   ◉ as viewers

jktechwriter@gmail.com

Separate email addresses with commas.
Choose from contacts

Invite viewers

Figure 5-16. *Invite others to view your document without worrying about them making changes.*

The recipient of your invite will receive an email (see Figure 5-17) and can click a link to view the file.

Lorem ipsum dolor sit amet, consectet...   Inbox | x

lovemynetbook@gmail.com to me

I've shared a document with you called "Lorem ipsum dolor sit amet, consectet...":
http://docs.google.com/Doc?id=dgsk5g5r_08kwpjzf7&invite=276611374

It's not an attachment -- it's stored online at Google Docs. To open this document, just click the link above.
---

check it out

Figure 5-17. *Those you share your document with will receive an email with a link to the file.*

Inviting collaborators is identical to inviting viewers. The only difference is whether you want to give collaborators the ability to invite others. To prevent this, uncheck the box labeled "Collaborators may invite others" before clicking the button that says, "Invite collaborators."

You can remove any viewer or collaborator at any time by clicking the X to the right of given person's email address, as shown in Figure 5-18.

Whether sharing or publishing your files, Google Docs makes it easy to turn these features off and on. Sharing and Publishing are great ways to get feedback on any files you create using Google Docs, including

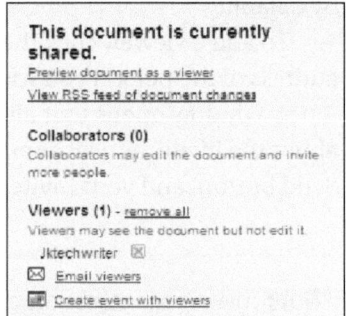

This document is currently shared.
Preview document as a viewer
View RSS feed of document changes

Collaborators (0)
Collaborators may edit the document and invite more people.

Viewers (1) - remove all
Viewers may see the document but not edit it.
Jktechwriter ⊠
⊠ Email viewers
▦ Create event with viewers

Figure 5-18. *Remove viewers and collaborators easily.*

spreadsheets and slideshows. Now let's take a quick look at both Google Docs Spreadsheet and Google Docs Presentation.

By the way, if you have a Google Docs file on your hard drive that you'd like to upload (and possibly share with others), simply click the Upload button (see Figure 5-8) on the Google Docs main page and browse to the location of the file. Simple!

Note Keep in mind that Publishing and Sharing options work the same for Google Docs Spreadsheet and Google Docs Presentation. For both a spreadsheet and a slideshow, you can publish your file to the web for anyone to see or use the sharing feature to limit who can view and make changes to a file.

Google Docs Spreadsheet and Presentation

Return to the Google Docs homepage (refer back to Figure 5-4), click the New menu, and select Spreadsheet. A blank Spreadsheet file will open in a new browser window or a tab like the one shown in Figure 5-19.

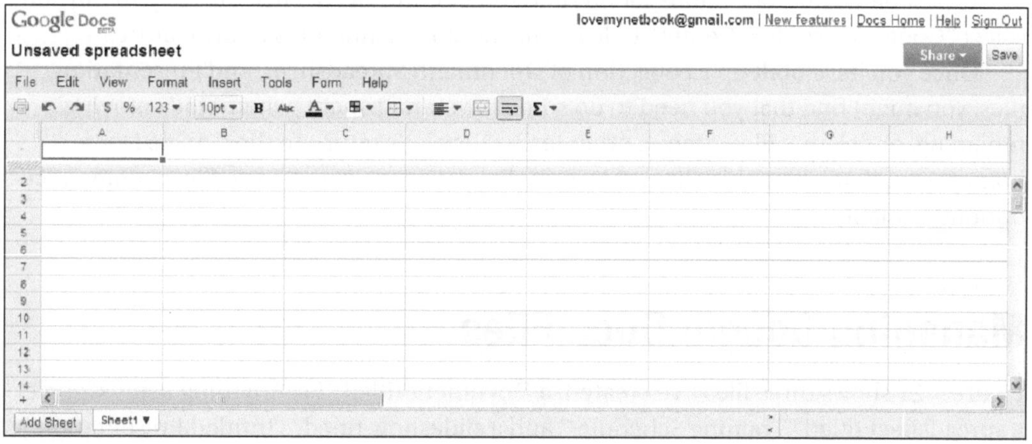

Figure 5-19. *Google Docs Spreadsheet is a powerful but easy-to-use spreadsheet app.*

Just like Google Docs Document, Spreadsheet offers a variety of features in its menus and toolbar. If you are new to using spreadsheets, I highly recommend that you click the Help menu and choose "Google Docs Help Center" to learn all about the features included in Spreadsheet. Besides performing calculations, Spreadsheet also has the ability to create graphs and charts, all of which can be published to the Web or shared with others.

To create a new slideshow, return to the Google Docs homepage, click New, and select Presentation. A blank Presentation file will open as shown in Figure 5-20.

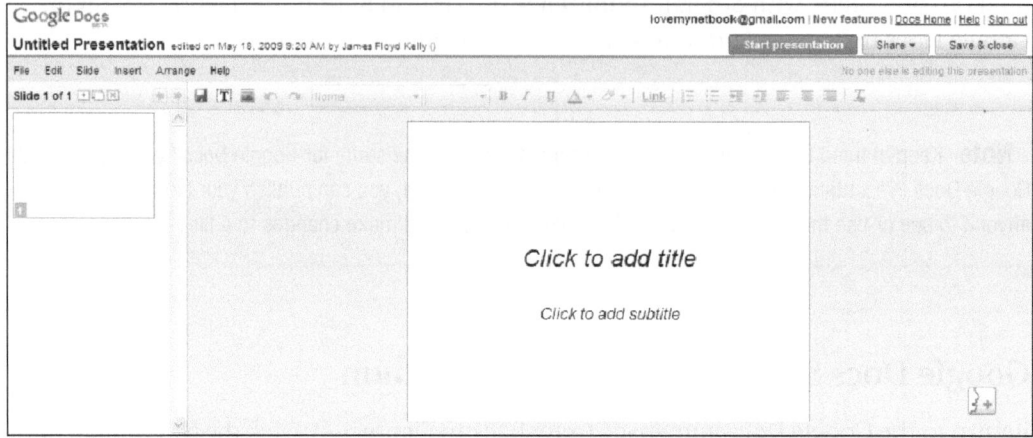

Figure 5-20. *Google Docs Presentation lets you create slideshows effortlessly.*

Experiment with the various menus and toolbar buttons or click the Help menu and select "Google Docs Help Center" to learn all about Presentation's many features.

Once you have built up a collection of Document, Spreadsheet, and Presentation files, you might find that you need to do some file management, whether it's moving, renaming, or deleting files, among other tasks. Now let's return to the Google Docs homepage; I'll finish up this chapter by showing you some of the basic file-maintenance options available.

Managing Google Docs Files

Figure 5-21 shows three files I've created: a Document titled "Fix Anything using Google," a spreadsheet titled "Training Schedule," and a slideshow titled "Untitled Presentation."

Let's start off by renaming the slideshow to something a little more descriptive. Whenever you want to perform an action on a file (such as rename, delete, and so on), you first need to place a check next to the file, as shown in Figure 5-22.

Next, click the Rename button; the file's name is highlighted, so it's simply matter of making your changes (see Figure 5-23) and clicking the Enter button when you're done.

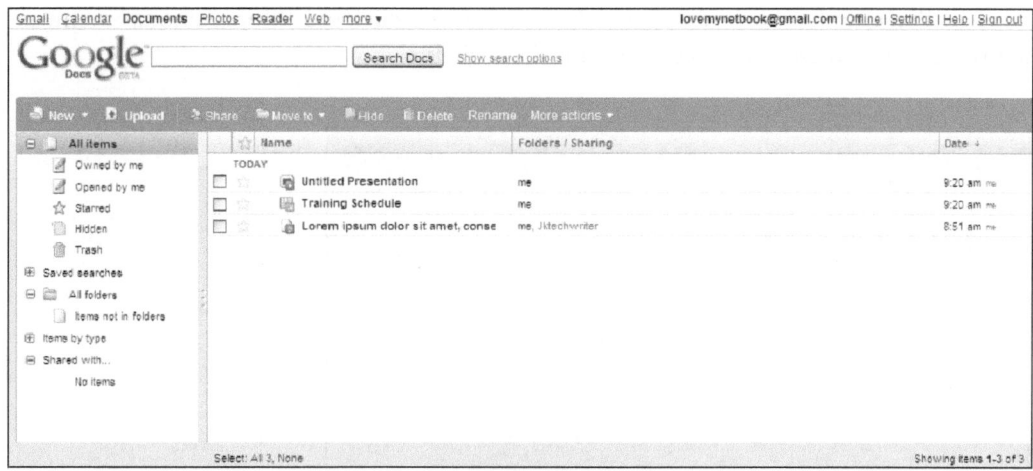

Figure 5-21. *Manage all of your Google Docs files easily.*

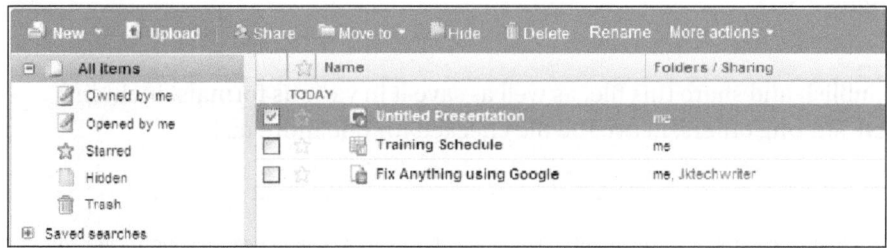

Figure 5-22. *Select the file(s) that you wish to perform an action on.*

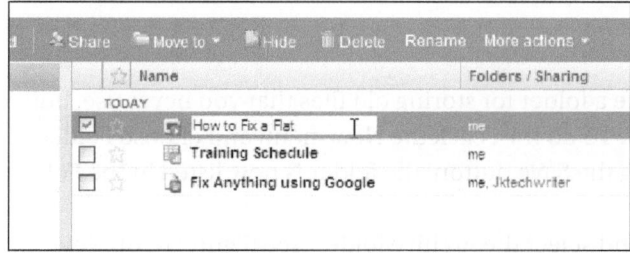

Figure 5-23. *Renaming a file to make it more descriptive*

The Presentation file is left checked for now; if you click the "More Actions" menu as shown in Figure 5-24, you can see other tasks available.

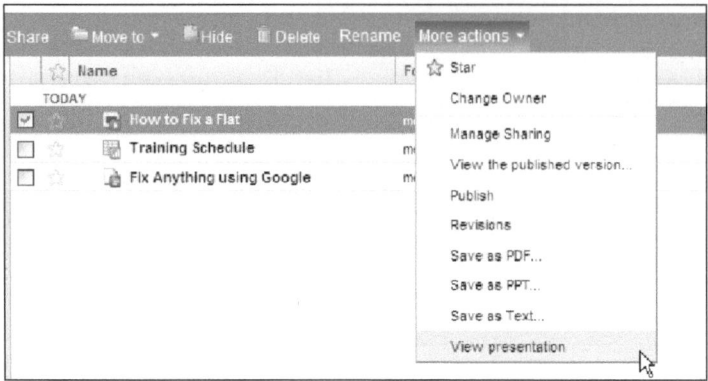

Figure 5-24. *The More Actions menu lets you perform even more tasks with your Google Docs files.*

You can publish and share this file, as well as save it in various formats, including HTML and PDF, among others. Leave the file checked for one more task.

Tip If you'd like to give control of a document to someone else (with a Google user account), click the Change Owner selection and enter the new owner's user name (the Google user account name). Type a quick message if you want and click the button that says, "Change owner." Your status will change to collaborator unless the new owner changes your status to viewer or removes your access entirely.

Let's assume you'd like to create a folder for storing old files that you never use, but would still like to keep (just in case). To do this, click the New menu and choose Folder. After naming the folder and clicking the Save button, the folder is now listed in the Folder window (see Figure 5-25).

Next, click the Move to menu and select the Archive folder (see Figure 5-26). Now click the button that says "Move to folder" that relocates the slideshow titled, "How to Fix a Flat" to the Archive folder.

There are many more options available to you when it comes to file management; hiding, deleting, changing ownership, and even uploading an existing file from your netbook's hard drive to Google Docs. (Consult the Help documentation for more details on how to perform these actions.)

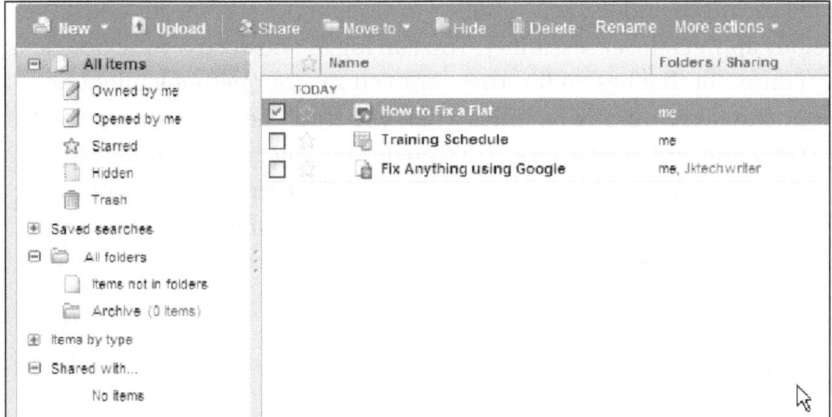

Figure 5-25. *Create folders to help organize your Google Docs files.*

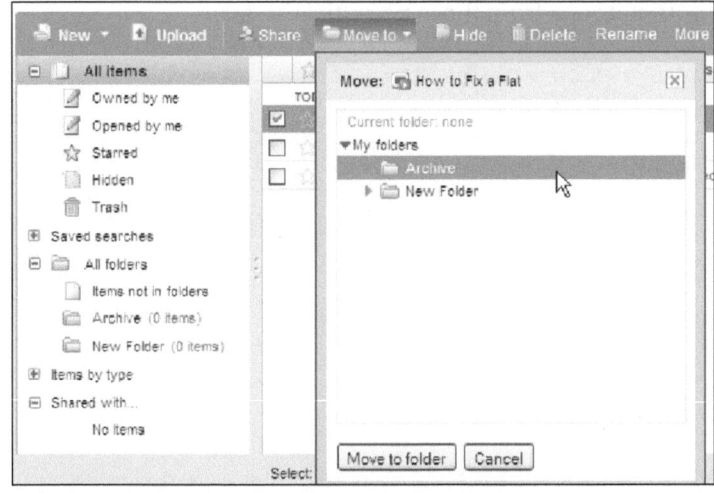

Figure 5-26. *Move a file to a folder using the "Move to" menu.*

Believe it or not, Google Docs is still considered by many to be in its infancy. It doesn't have nearly the number of features available in more established applications (such as Microsoft Word, Excel, or PowerPoint), but that's not necessarily a bad thing. Google is always updating Google Docs by adding new features and making it even easier to use. Advantages include the ability to organize all your files using one application (a browser, at that), seamless integration with other Google services like Sites, and, of course, 24/7 availability from any computer with an Internet connection.

But if you're not convinced about the usefulness of Google Docs, consider one more feature that I especially appreciate: accessibility. You can log in and access your Google Docs files from any computer that has an Internet connection. Your netbook might be small and lightweight, but there will still be times when you won't be able to bring your netbook with you. If you find you need access to a Google Docs file, any computer with a browser and Internet connection will work in a pinch. Combine this with the ability to share and publish your files, and Google Docs is one cloud computing application that you might discover to be indispensable.

What's Next?

While you're uploading and downloading files to and from your netbook over the Internet, you should take a moment and make sure that your netbook is protected from some of the nasty stuff floating out there. I'm talking about viruses and spyware, and Chapter 6 will show you how to protect your netbook from those potential threats.

CHAPTER 6

■ ■ ■

Netbook Malware Protection

Malicious software is everywhere, whether it's viruses, worms, or spyware. Some of this software is meant to spy on you, tracking your keystrokes and online purchases. Other types of software seek to crash your operating system or delete your important files. Whatever the purpose of these types of malicious software (often referred to as malware), the fact is that such software exists and, unless you take the right precautions, it will find its way to your new netbook.

Your netbook might be small, lightweight, and extremely fun to use, but it's still a computer and subject to the same risks that larger computers face. And don't think you're protected because you never download any software of "unknown origin," transfer files from a USB flash drive, or click unfamiliar links from the Internet; if your device connects to the Internet, it's at risk from viruses, spyware, and other not-so-friendly applications that need only a live Internet connection to make the jump to your netbook.

This chapter will cover three ways for you to protect your Windows netbook. The first involves installing and using antivirus software; no computer should be without this protection. Second, I'll cover an anti-spyware application that I highly recommend you also install and use regularly. And third, I'll tackle Microsoft Update, which I'll show you how to configure on your Windows operating system, so it can protect itself automatically with software updates released by Microsoft.

Don't take chances with your netbook. Turn on your netbook, connect to the Internet, and follow my instructions to get some immediate protection for your computer. When you finish this chapter, your netbook will be armed with some powerful tools to help it fight future malware attacks.

Antivirus Protection

Computer viruses are never fun. A small number of them might do nothing more evil than replace your computer screen's wallpaper with something like a funny picture (or possibly an offensive picture), leaving your valuable files and operating system intact (if you're lucky). But a large portion of viruses out there have one goal—to do as much damage as possible: damage to your files, damage to your operating system, and damage to your free time when you discover that you have to reinstall your operating system and applications. Worse, you might have to pay money to have your deleted files recovered (which can run $1,000 or more).

To make matters worse, new viruses are released every day. Many of them are variations of existing viruses (mutations in geek-speak), but many have never been seen before by the computer experts that monitor these things (because they're often variations, an updated antivirus program will typically catch them anyway). Antivirus software is the chief weapon used to fight back against computer viruses. Most antivirus applications are designed to download a special virus update file on a regular basis (monthly, weekly, and in some cases, even daily). This special file contains instructions for the antivirus application that tell it how to identify all known viruses and how to clean them up. If you have an antivirus application installed on your computer and that application self-updates by downloading this special file frequently, you're already ahead of the game. But if you're not running an antivirus app, your netbook is a potential target just waiting for a virus to strike.

You have many choices when it comes to antivirus applications. There are dozens of antivirus programs that you can purchase at the store and install on your netbook. Most commercial antivirus apps give you a one-year subscription that allows the application to download the virus-update file. When the subscription ends, you pay a fee and renew it so you can keep your computer's antivirus software up-to-date.

But this isn't the only solution. There are plenty of free antivirus applications out there that work just as well and have no subscription fee.

Whether you want to pay for an antivirus application or download and install a free one, the important thing is to do it now—don't wait for disaster to strike.

Antivirus Apps for Netbooks

I'll cover two antivirus alternatives here that are great for netbooks. One requires that you install an application on your netbook, while the other is a cloud computing service that does all the good stuff behind the scenes while you're connected to the Internet (and later, when disconnected). You can also install both, but it's not necessary.

ClamWin

The ClamWin antivirus application doesn't require much in terms of hard drive space, nor does it put a lot of demand on your netbook's processor. To begin installing it, open your Internet browser and visit www.clamwin.com (see Figure 6-1).

Figure 6-1. *ClamWin is a free antivirus application that's perfect for netbooks.*

Click the Download link along the left edge of the screen and then click the Download Now button to save the installation file to your netbook's hard drive. After the installation file is downloaded, double-click the file to launch the Antivirus Setup Wizard (see Figure 6-2). Click the Next button to continue.

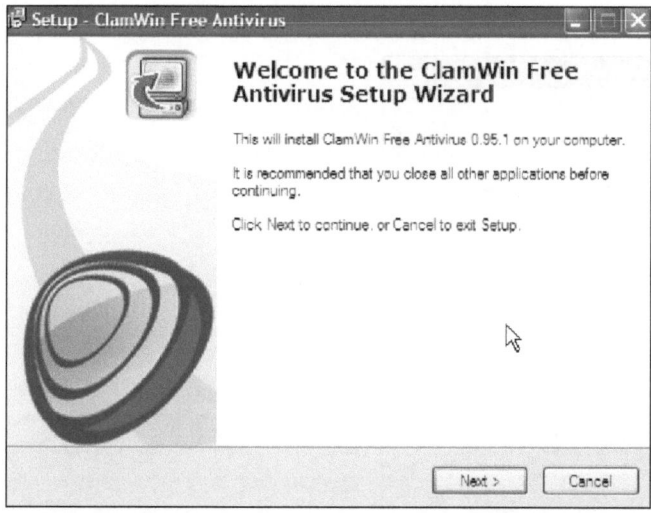

Figure 6-2. *ClamWin has a setup wizard to guide you through the installation.*

Read through the License Agreement; if the terms are acceptable to you, select the "I Accept the Agreement" option and click Next as shown in Figure 6-3.

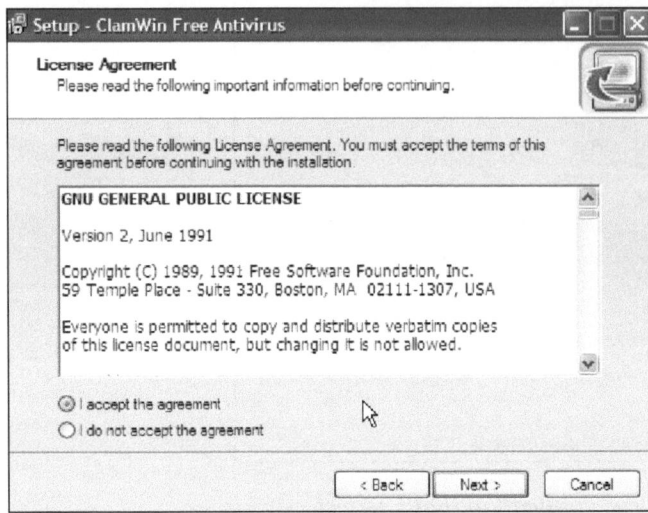

Figure 6-3. *The ClamWin Free Antivirus license agreement*

Figure 6-4 shows a screen that asks you who will use the antivirus application. By default, the "Anyone who uses this computer" option is selected. I recommend you select the former, but if you have multiple user accounts on your netbook, you can choose the "Only for me" option and allow the other users to install the antivirus application of their choice. Click the Next button to continue.

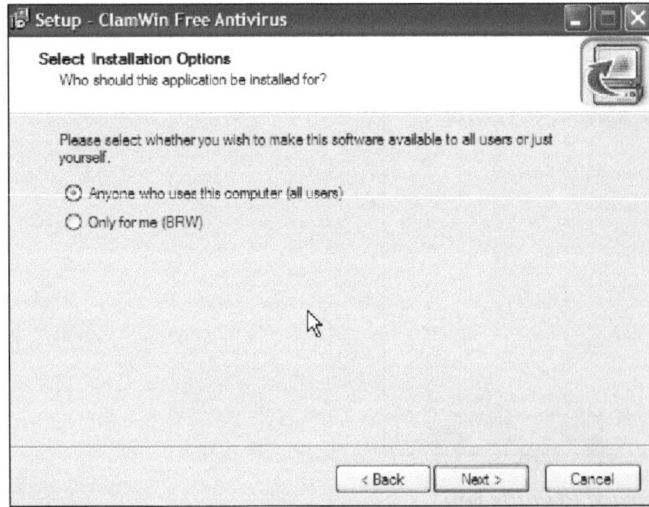

Figure 6-4. *Choose which user accounts ClamWin will protect.*

The next screen shown allows you to specify the location where ClamWin will be installed (see Figure 6-5). I recommend that you accept the default location and click the Next button; click the Browse button if you wish to install the application elsewhere.

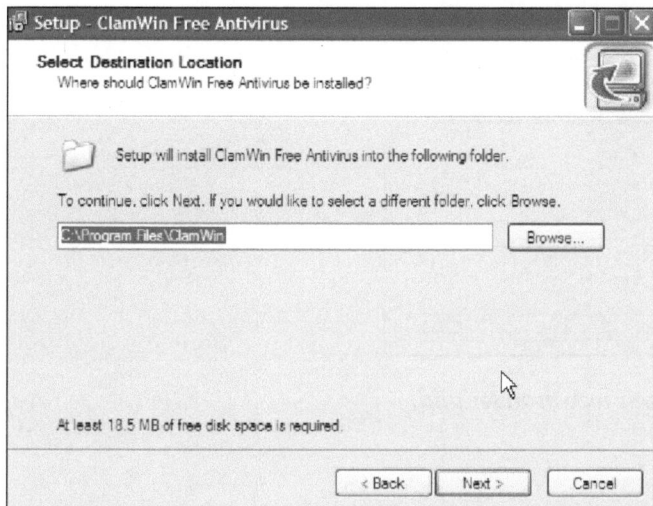

Figure 6-5. *ClamWin will be installed in the Program Files folder by default.*

The Select Components screen is shown in Figure 6-6. You can choose optional language support (currently only English, Dutch, and French), as well as whether ClamWin can scan incoming and outgoing emails from Microsoft Outlook. (I don't use Outlook, so I've deselected the "Integration with Microsoft Outlook" option.)

Another option to consider here is whether ClamWin will protect your web browser. Internet Explorer (IE) comes standard with most Windows operating systems, but I prefer to use Firefox as my default browser, so I've turned off this option. If you ever anticipate that you might need to use Internet Explorer, I'd suggest leaving the option checked; it could be that someone using your computer is more familiar with IE and selects it from the Start button. Whatever the reason, it can't hurt to leave this option checked. Click the Next button to continue.

Next, you're given the option to choose where ClamWin will place the application's launch icon in the Start menu. I recommend leaving the default location and clicking the Next button, but feel free to click the Browse button and change the location if you like.

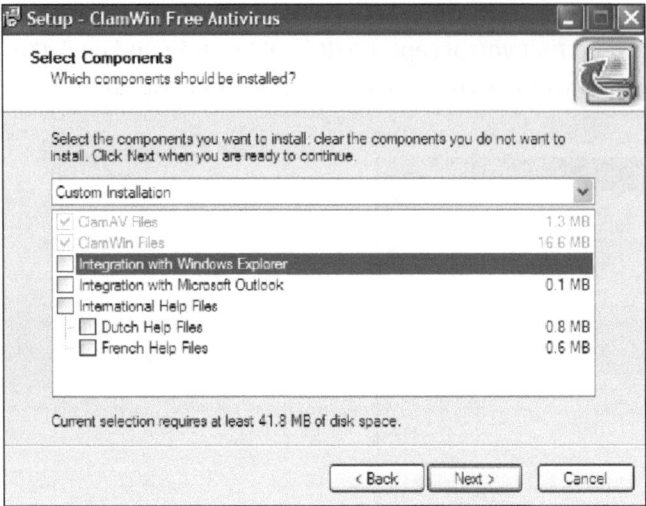

Figure 6-6. *ClamWin can protect your web browser and Microsoft Outlook.*

Figure 6-7 shows the next screen, where you are asked if you'd like to download the latest virus update files (highly recommended) and whether you'd like to create a desktop icon. Make your selections and click the Next button.

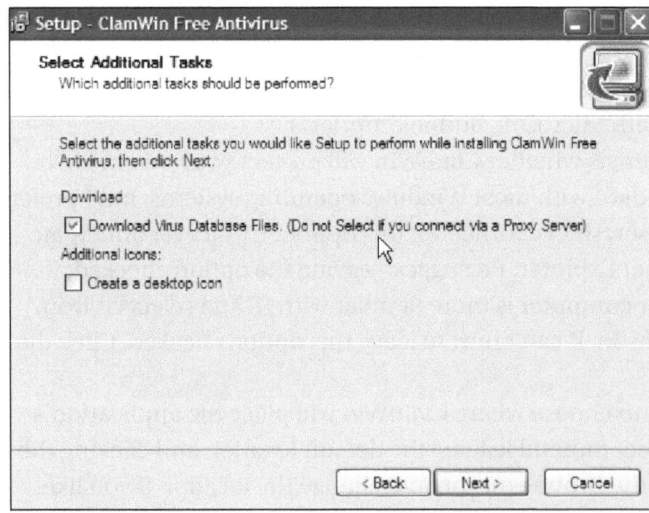

Figure 6-7. *Walk through a few more tasks that you select or ignore, and ClamWin is almost ready to install.*

The next screen provides a summary of all your selections. Click the Back button to go back and make any changes or click the Install button, and ClamWin will finish its installation. If you elected for the virus update files to be downloaded, you'll see those files downloading during the install. Click the Finish button when done.

To run ClamWin, click the Start button, select the ClamWin Antivirus group, and then click Virus Scanner as shown in Figure 6-8.

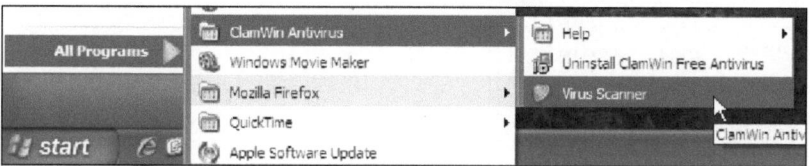

Figure 6-8. *Run ClamWin by selecting it from the Start menu.*

Figure 6-9 shows the simple interface provided by ClamWin, along with some of the buttons you use to configure how ClamWin works.

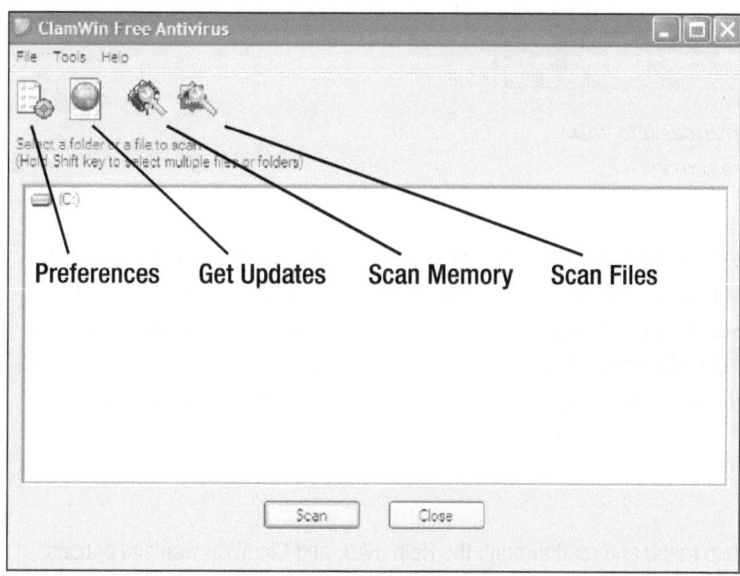

Figure 6-9. *ClamWin's basic interface is simple-to-use and easy-to-configure.*

The Help menu provides much more detail on using ClamWin, and I highly encourage you to read through the documentation. In the meantime, I'll walk you through two simple tasks to get you started. First, click the Preferences button in the upper-left corner and the ClamWin Preferences screen will open; click the Internet Updates tab as shown in Figure 6-10.

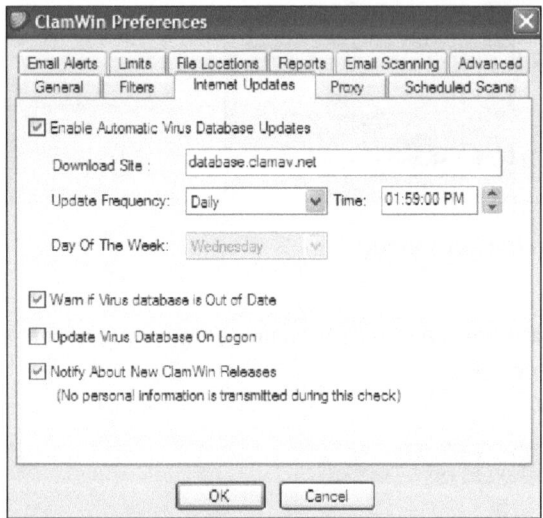

Figure 6-10. *ClamWin Preferences lets you customize how the software works.*

Make certain that the "Enable Automatic Virus Database Updates" box is checked; if it's not, ClamWin cannot get the latest updates and protect your netbook against the newest viruses. Choose your update frequency from the drop-down menu (the default is Daily) and set the time for the download to begin. You can check or uncheck the boxes at the bottom of the screen to receive or ignore alerts from ClamWin. Click the OK button when done.

Tip Be sure to click on the Help menu and read through the Help, FAQ, and ClamWin web site options; you'll learn how to use your new antivirus application better and keep your netbook safe.

All that remains is to perform a basic virus scan of your netbook. Select the drive letter for your hard drive (C:, for example), click the Scan button, and the scan will begin. Figure 6-11 shows that my scan was successfully completed and one infected file was found. Depending on how many files you have and the size and speed of your hard drive, this could take a few minutes or an hour or longer.

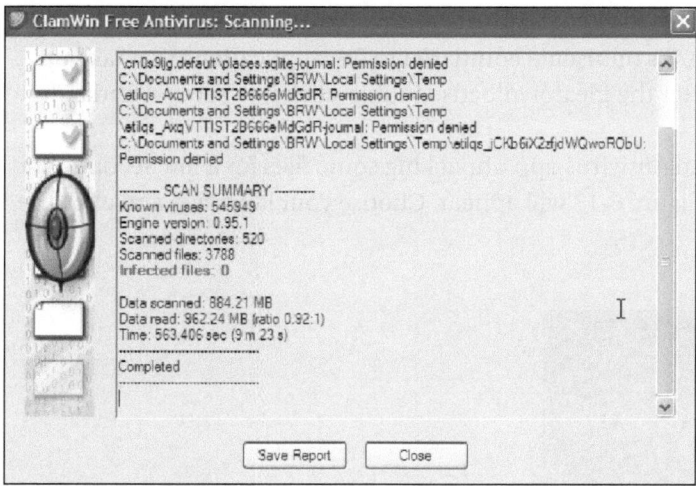

Figure 6-11. *ClamWin gives you a report when it finishes scanning your files.*

As I mentioned earlier in the chapter, ClamWin isn't your only option for an antivirus application. If you like the idea of cloud computing, then you're likely to find the next antivirus service very appealing.

Panda Cloud Antivirus

You can find the Panda Cloud Antivirus application by visiting www.cloudantivirus.com (see Figure 6-12).

Figure 6-12. *Panda Cloud Antivirus is a low-maintenance but powerful solution for netbooks.*

Click the Download button and save the file to your hard drive. (Yes, there is a small file that must be installed, but it's miniscule compared to full applications that take up valuable hard drive space.) After the file downloads, double-click it to set up Panda Cloud Antivirus.

You'll see the Panda Cloud Antivirus app unpacking some files for a few seconds and then a screen like the one in Figure 6-13 will appear. Choose your language and click the Next button.

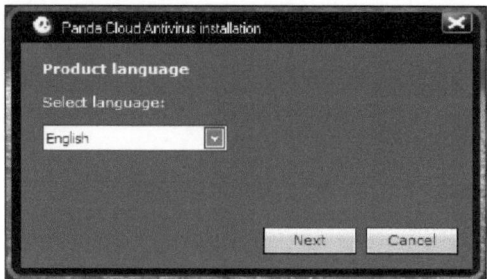

Figure 6-13. *The Panda Cloud Antivirus installation begins.*

Click the License agreement link to read the rules related to using this application (see Figure 6-14).

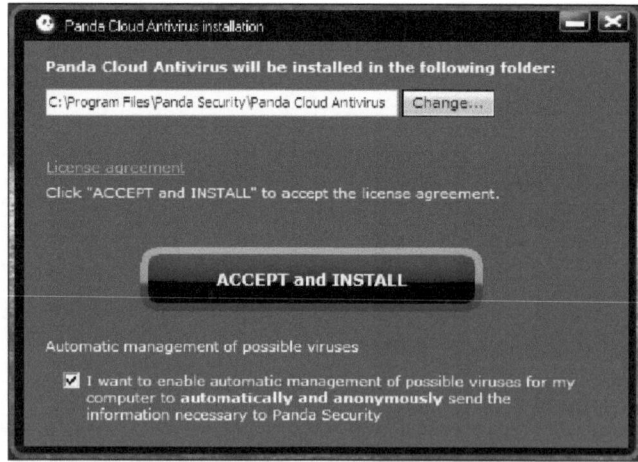

Figure 6-14. *The Panda Cloud Antivirus License Agreement screen*

Pay attention to the text at the bottom of the window in Figure 6-14. By leaving the box checked, you are allowing your netbook to send information to Panda whenever your netbook is connected to the Internet. This allows Panda to manage your antivirus application for you—this is the "cloud computing" aspect of the deal. The information sent is anonymous and related to your netbook's "vitals," and it includes information about your netbook's processor, RAM, and hard drive statistics during the operation of the application.

None of your personal files will be sent over, so no worries. (But if this approach does bother you, then by all means close down the installer and delete the installation file from your netbook). If you uncheck the box and continue the installation, you will be responsible for updating the application and scanning for viruses versus the application doing it for you automatically.

Click the Accept and Install button to continue; when the installation is complete, click the Finish button. You should notice a small Panda icon in the lower left corner as shown in Figure 6-15.

Figure 6-15. *The Panda icon lets you know the antivirus application is running.*

Double-click the Panda icon, and a small window like the one in Figure 6-16 will open.

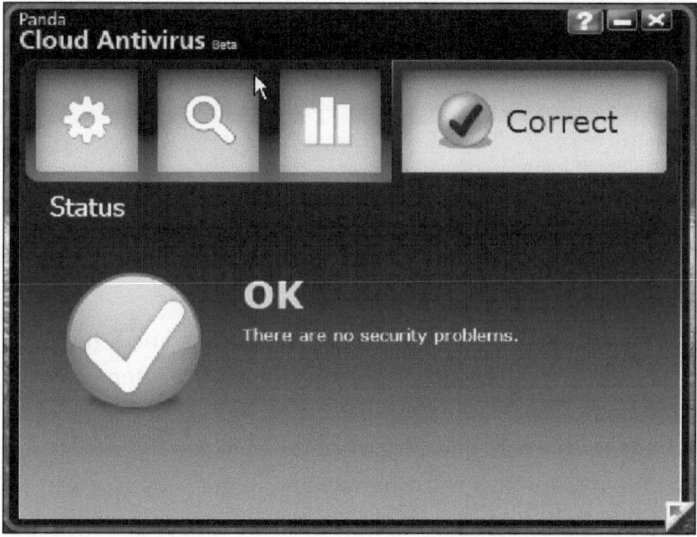

Figure 6-16. *The big green check tells you everything is OK.*

Click the tab with the Gear icon. You can disable the "Automatic management of possible viruses" or enable this feature if you chose to turn this feature off initially.

Next, click the tab with the magnifying glass icon (see Figure 6-17).

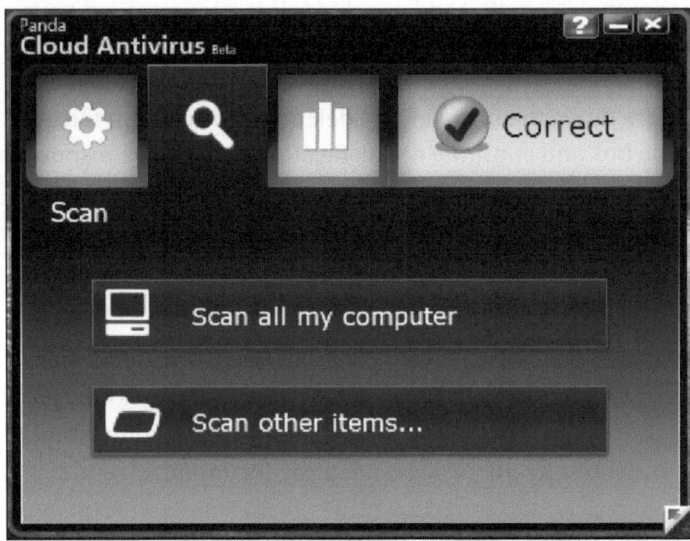

Figure 6-17. *You can scan your netbook whenever you like or let Panda handle it for you.*

Click the "Scan all my computer" option if you'd like to scan your netbook's entire hard drive. Or, you can take the less time-intensive route by clicking the "Scan other items" option to select individual files, folders, or even pen drives to scan.

Finally, click the tab with the bars (see Figure 6-18).

From here, you can monitor how many viruses and other malware instances have been caught and removed. As you can see, my netbook is clean as a whistle after a complete hard drive scan (see Figure 6-17).

ClamWin and Panda Cloud Antivirus work differently, but they ultimately perform the same service: protecting your netbook from malware. In addition to these two apps, you read about a side-by-side comparison of other antivirus apps by visiting www.av-comparatives.org. The most important thing: Make sure you use whichever antivirus application you choose to install.

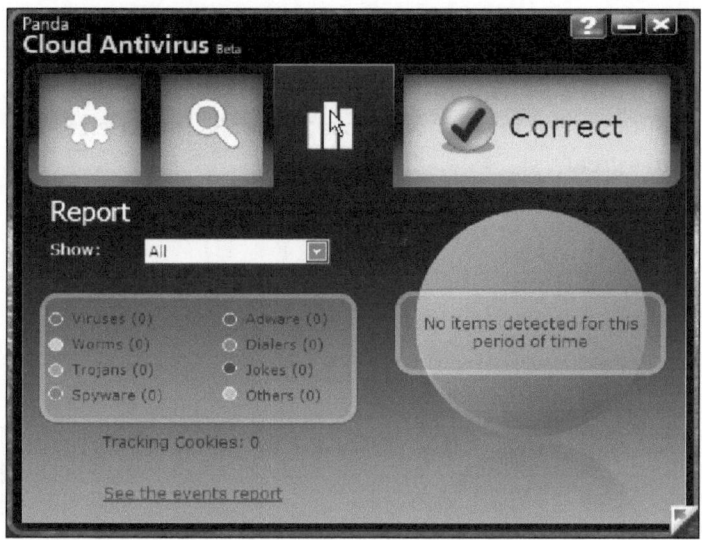

Figure 6-18. *Check the status of scans by Panda Cloud Antivirus on your netbook.*

Anti-spyware Protection

Viruses are annoying, but they are only one of several threats you face as a netbook owner. One of the most annoying software developments in the past 10 years or so has to be spyware. These little applications are always finding their way onto your computer, mainly via your web browser, but they also hitch rides on legitimate software you purchase and install. When you visit certain web sites or install some applications, little pieces of software are secretly installed on your netbook that keep track of all kinds of things: web sites you visit, credit cards you favor, and even what types of music and books you read.

Note Not all of this tracking is necessarily bad—Amazon.com, for example, uses a small tracking file called a cookie that does nothing more than provide the company with the ability to know who you are when you return to the web site and offers up recommendations to you based on past purchases. For more information on cookies and how they work (and why you shouldn't fear them), visit `http://en.wikipedia.org/wiki/HTTP_cookie`.

Spyware isn't going away, so the best solution is to take a hint from the antivirus applications and install something that can help you find and remove the spyware that's been added to your netbook's hard drive. As with antivirus applications, there are products you can purchase and free options. For my netbook, I use Spybot S&D (Search & Destroy), a free solution that works great.

SpyBot S&D

Visit www.safer-networking.org and click your desired language to view the screen shown in Figure 6-19.

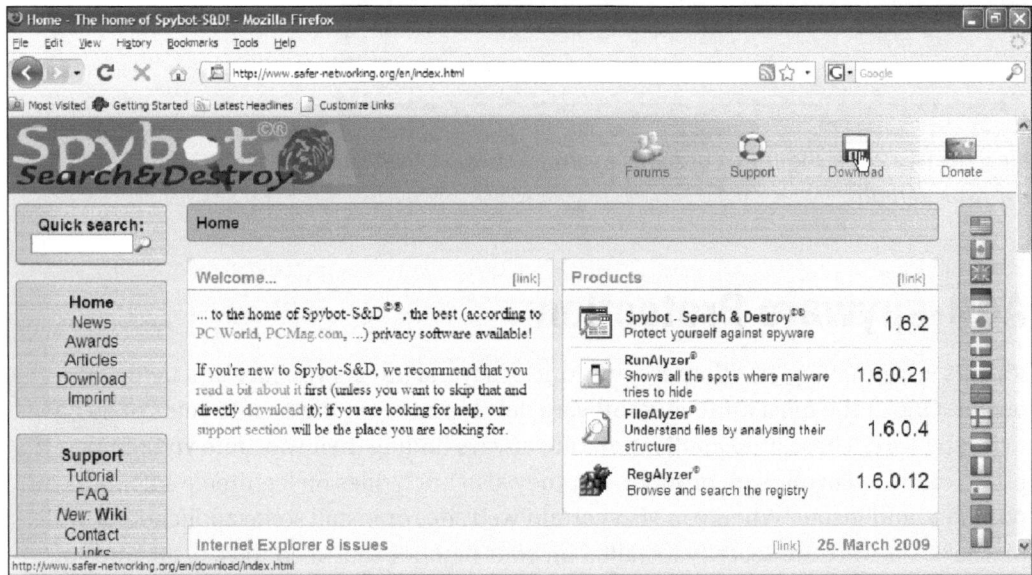

Figure 6-19. *Spybot S&D can protect your netbook from spyware.*

Click the Download link in the upper-right corner, then scroll down the page and click the "Spybot – Search & Destroy" link or the Download button and follow the instructions to download the installation file to your netbook's hard drive. (Feel free to come back to this screen and make a donation if you find the application extremely helpful; this will help support the developers of the application and ensure its continued development.)

After you download the installation file, double-click it to start the installation. Select your language from the drop-down list shown in Figure 6-20 and click the OK button to continue.

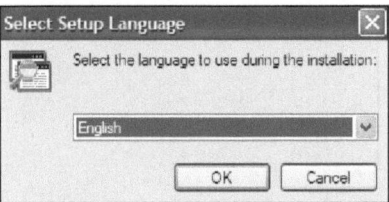

Figure 6-20. *The Spybot S&D setup begins with selecting the language for the installation.*

Click the Next button on the Setup Wizard screen to begin the installation. Read through the License Agreement and, after selecting the "I accept the agreement" option, click Next. Figure 6-21 shows the next screen, which lets you designate the location where the Spybot S&D files will be installed. Click the Browse button to choose a different location or leave the default location and click the Next button.

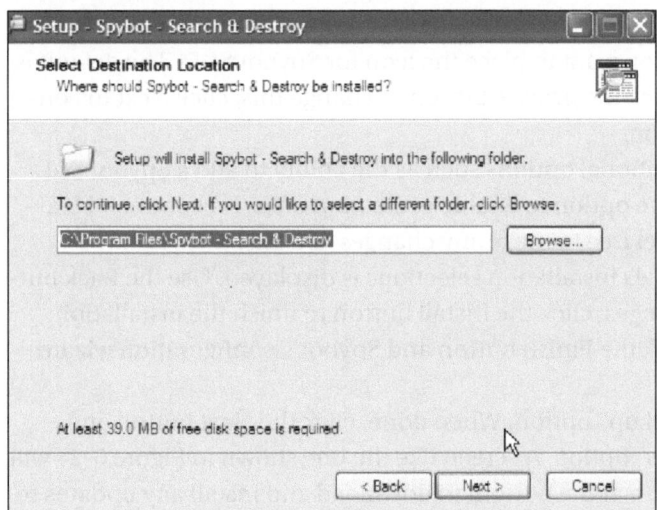

Figure 6-21. *The Spybot S&D Setup lets you decide where to install the application.*

On the next screen (see Figure 6-22), you can choose to install or deselect certain options for Spybot. I suggest you leave the default settings as they are, with the exception of "Additional languages"; uncheck that box and click Next.

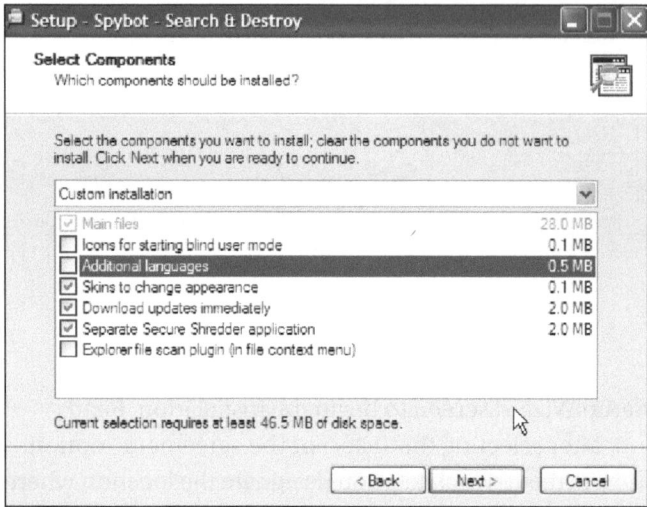

Figure 6-22. *The Spybot S&D Setup wizard lets you enable and disable a handful of options.*

The next screen asks where you want to place the icon for Spybot S&D. The default is in the Start menu, but you can click the Browse button to change this; click Next to continue after you make your selection.

You will be offered some additional options such as the ability to add a Spybot S&D icon to your desktop, as well as the option to enable protection of IE. I recommend leaving these options checked, but feel free to make any changes you like. Click Next.

A summary of your Spybot S&D installation selections is displayed. Use the Back button to go back and make any changes; click the Install button to finish the installation. When the install is complete, click the Finish button and Spybot's configuration wizard will open (see Figure 6-23).

Click the "Create registry backup" option. When done, click the Next button and then click the "Search for updates" option. A screen like the one shown in Figure 6-24 will appear. Click the Download button at the bottom to download and install any updates to Spybot S&D. Spybot might shut down and restart for some updates.

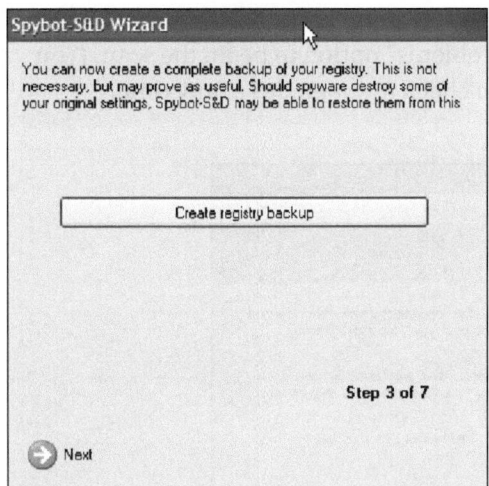

Figure 6-23. *The Spybot S&D configuration wizard opens.*

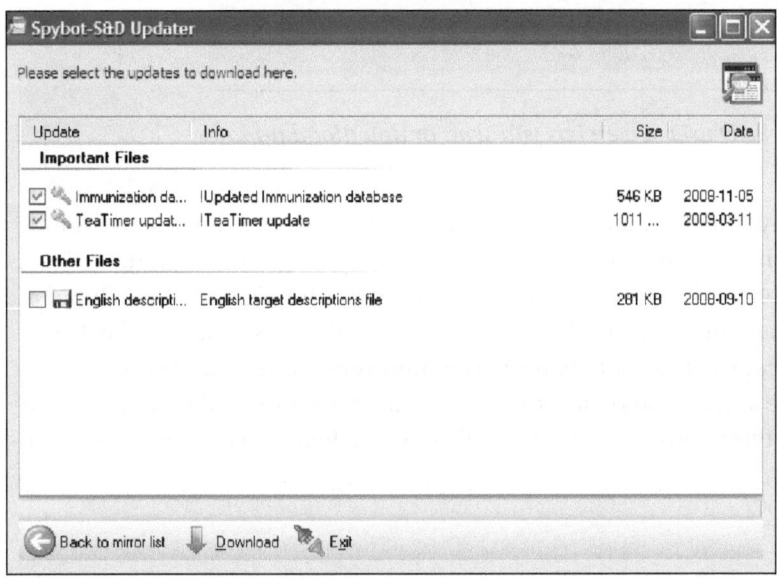

Figure 6-24. *The Spybot S&D Updater will download any available updates.*

After updates are complete, the Spybot S&D application is ready for you to scan your system (see Figure 6-25). Click the "Check for problems" option to begin the scan. (You can also click the "Search for Updates" option to check for upgrades at any time.)

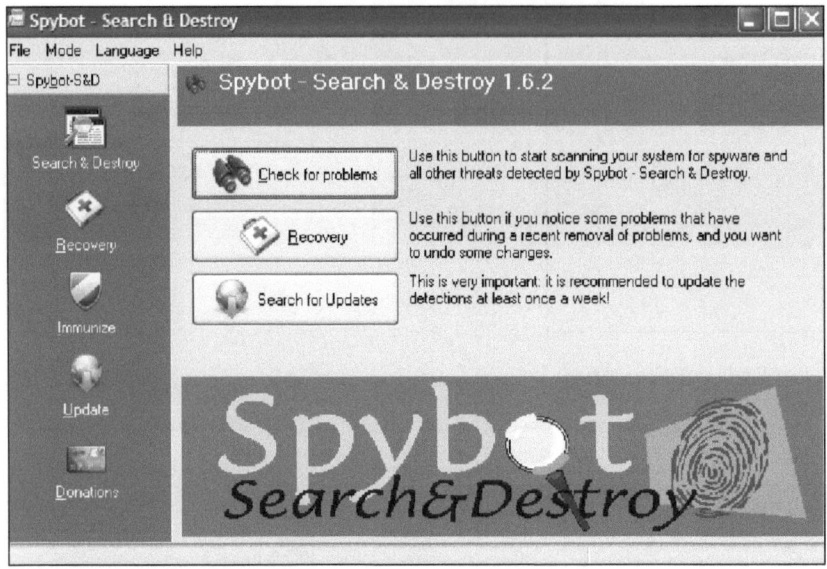

Figure 6-25. *The Spybot S&D user screen lets you scan or download updates.*

A status bar displays the download's progress along the bottom of Spybot's window (see Figure 6-26). When the scan is complete, Spybot lists any spyware it found.

Spybot S&D is a great little application for your netbook, and it's 100% free. But it's not the only free spyware removal tool that's popular. You might also want to check out Ad-Aware Free at www.lavasoft.com. Many users run both versions with no conflict!

Now that you have antivirus and anti-spyware applications installed and running to protect your netbook, there's just one more task I'll cover to help you lock down and protect your netbook.

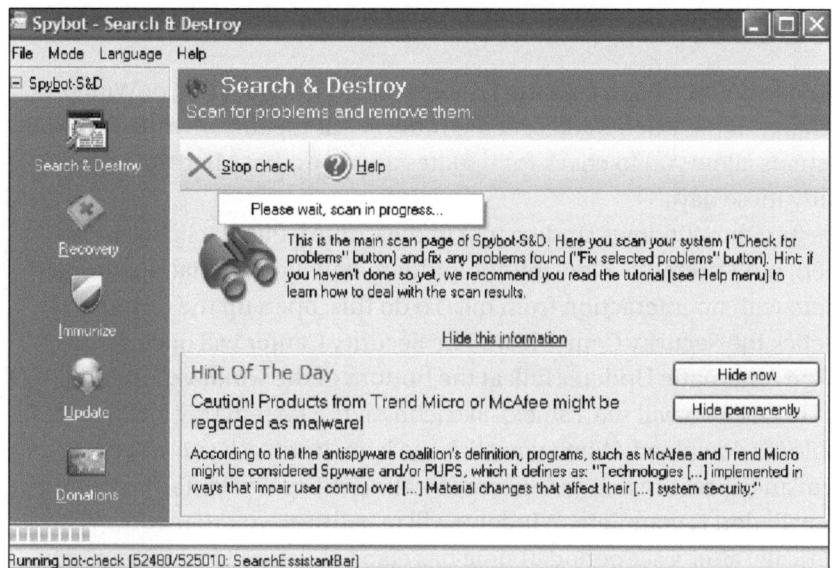

Figure 6-26. *The Spybot S&D scan looks for all sorts of spyware and offers to fix what it finds.*

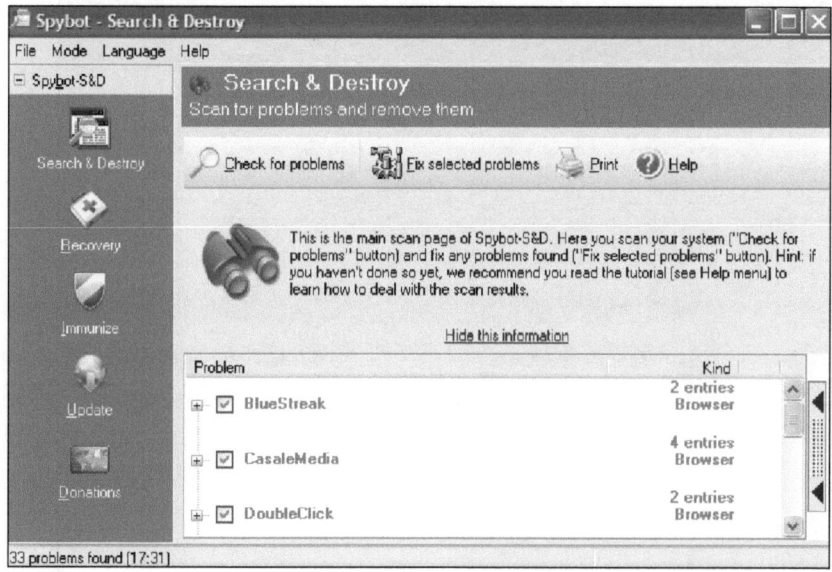

Figure 6-27. *Remove spyware that's been installed on your netbook.*

Microsoft Update

It doesn't really matter whether you're running Windows XP, Windows Vista, or Windows 7 (this name might change later, but it's still called Windows 7 at the time I write this)—all three operating systems allow you to check for updates and fixes that Microsoft releases somewhat frequently these days.

You can always find the Windows Update tool in the Control Panel (click Start and select Control Panel), but I prefer to allow my computer to download updates automatically and install them with no interaction from me. To do this, open up the Control Panel and double-click the Security Center icon. The Security Center will open (see Figure 6-28); click the Automatic Updates link at the bottom of the window. When Automatic Update is set to ON, you will see a shield-like icon on the system tray when there are updates available for download. When you click the icon, it will ask you whether you want to perform an Express Install or Custom Install. The Express Install is the best choice. Once an installation is complete, Windows will usually ask you to reboot (Vista will reboot automatically after a set period of time has elapsed—usually when you're in the middle of a great game of Peggle).

Figure 6-28. *Automatic Updates lets you download new features and fixes to your operating system.*

The Automatic Updates window will open as shown in Figure 6-29. If the "Automatic (recommended)" option isn't selected, click it. You can then choose how often the check occurs (every day or a specific day), as well as the time for any available updates to be downloaded. Keep in mind that your computer must be turned on for this to happen. Figure 6-29 shows that my netbook will check for updates every night at 3 a.m.; this is fine because I leave my netbook running at night.

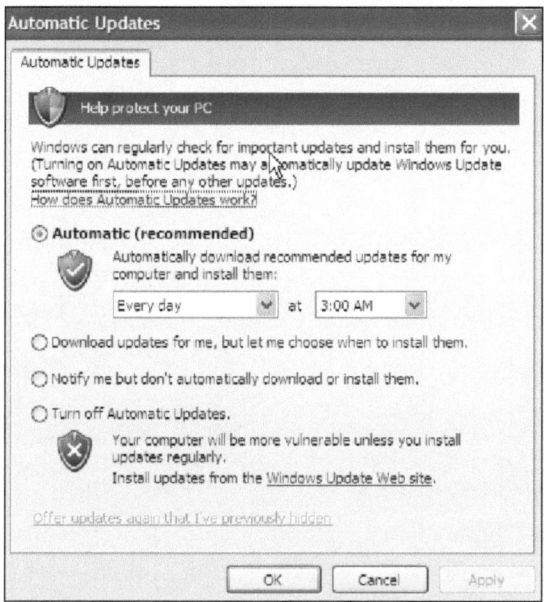

Figure 6-29. *Schedule automatic updates that are downloaded at your convenience.*

Click the OK button when you're done and then close down the Security Center and Control Panel. Your netbook is now being protected against viruses and spyware and will download updates from Microsoft automatically.

What's Next?

Your Windows netbook most likely came with Internet Explorer pre-installed as the default web browser, but this isn't your only option when it comes to browsing the Internet. I'd like to introduce you to two other web browsers that work great on a netbook. And if you should find that you like one of them better than Internet Explorer, I'm also going to show you how to remove IE and save some hard drive space.

CHAPTER 7

∎∎∎

Netbook Web Browsers

This book focuses on netbooks that come installed with the Microsoft Windows operating system. This also means that the default web browser installed on your new netbook is most likely Microsoft's Internet Explorer (IE). It's a good web browser, with all the standard features you'd expect from a browser: bookmarks (or Favorites), the ability to block pop-ups, and the ability to set your homepage are just a few examples of its features.

But Internet Explorer has some problems. First, because it's used by so many people, it always seems to be a target to hackers and other misfits who either try to damage the application with viruses or try to use it to hijack a user's computer. I can't count the number of times my Internet Explorer browser has crashed due to some strange malware attacking it; worse, it always seems to lock up when I need it the most. And how do all these extra toolbars always seem to find their way onto IE? There just always seems to be *something* going wrong with IE.

These days IE is always under attack. But uninstalling this Web browser can't be a good option, can it? In my particular case, I check my email using my web browser (see Chapter 8 on Gmail), I purchase a large percentage of my books from Amazon.com, and my browser gives me access to news, weather, and more.

Yes, a web browser is very important, but given the problems I've had with IE, I decided enough was enough. I've since switched to a completely different web browser (I'll introduce you to it shortly), and my browser-based Internet activities have become much more enjoyable.

Before I show you my two alternatives, however, let me first provide a quick overview of IE, so you'll be able to see some of the similarities and differences between IE and other browsers.

Internet Explorer

Internet Explorer probably needs no introduction; it's been the de facto standard for web browsers for more than a decade, and it comes built-in with all Windows operating system installations. Figure 7-1 shows the basic IE7 web browser.

Note By the time you read this, IE8 should be available; it will come standard with the Windows 7 operating system.

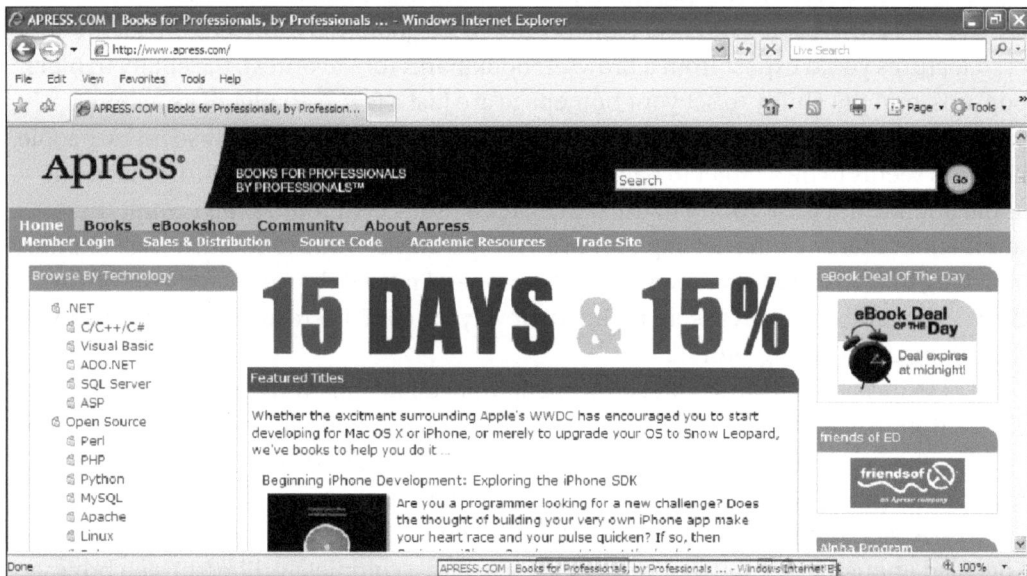

Figure 7-1. *The IE windows as viewed on a 10" netbook screen*

IE7 provides all the standard web browser toolbar buttons along its top edge, including Forward, Back, Stop, URL/web address field, and a search box. IE7 also provides you with the ability to view multiple web site pages in a tabbed format, instead of opening a new IE window for every web site you're visiting. Figure 7-2 shows a few web sites using the tabs feature.

Internet Explorer supports pop-up blocking, bookmarks, anti-phishing capabilities, and more. If you prefer to use IE and wish to learn more about the application, one of the best places to start is the Help menu; select "Internet Explorer Tour" to learn all about its basic features. You can also select "Online Support" to gain access to Microsoft's 100% free and searchable database of IE tips, tricks, and fixes.

Many people are 100% satisfied with the IE browser; if you like it, then by all means, continue to use it with your netbook. But if you're like me and love options, then continue reading to learn about two great alternatives to IE that will work great with your netbook.

REMOVING INTERNET EXPLORER FROM XP

If you'd like to remove Internet Explorer and gain back a small amount of hard drive space, click on the Start button, select Control Panel, and then double-click the Add/Remove Programs button. Make certain the "Show Updates" checkbox is unchecked, locate "Windows Internet Explorer 7," and click the Remove button. It's that simple! (For other operating systems, you'll need to consult Google—keep in mind, however, that IE7 and higher can be difficult to remove from Vista.)

Figure 7-2. *Tabs allow you to view multiple webpages from within one browser window.*

Firefox

One of the more popular alternative browsers out there is Firefox. It has the same basic features that you find in IE, but it also offers something called Add-ons that you're sure to enjoy (and that I'll talk about later). Figure 7-3 shows the basic Firefox browser; this is a screenshot taken directly from my netbook's 10" screen. Compare Figure 7-3 to Figure 7-4, which shows the same web site viewed from Firefox on my 17" laptop screen. Can you spot the difference?

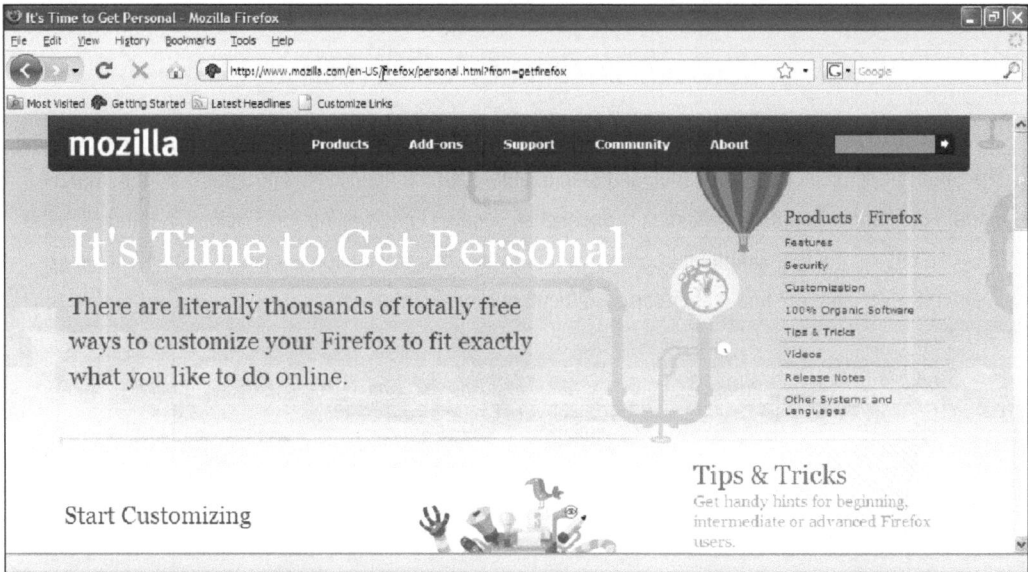

Figure 7-3. *The Firefox web browser home page as viewed on my 10" netbook screen*

Firefox can resize a web page to a point, but you'll find that large pages require a little more scrolling on a netbook. (This is one of the little sacrifices we netbook owners must make to enjoy carrying around our little two-pound wireless wonders.)

I highly recommend that you download and install Firefox and give it a spin. You can run multiple web browsers on your netbook with no worries; you might find, as I did, that you tend to favor one browser over another. If so, you can also choose to uninstall the "losing" browser and free up some valuable hard drive space—I'll show you how to remove IE at the end of the chapter, if you decide to switch to something else.

The first thing you'll need to do is open IE and visit www.getfirefox.com—scroll down just a little bit and click the big button labeled "Free Download" (see Figure 7-5). Note that the version number might be different than the one shown in the figure; just download the latest version and follow along with the steps provided.

After downloading the installation file, which takes less than two minutes using a WiFi connection, double-click the file to start the install by unpacking some files. You'll be greeted by the Setup Wizard shown in Figure 7-6. Click the Next button.

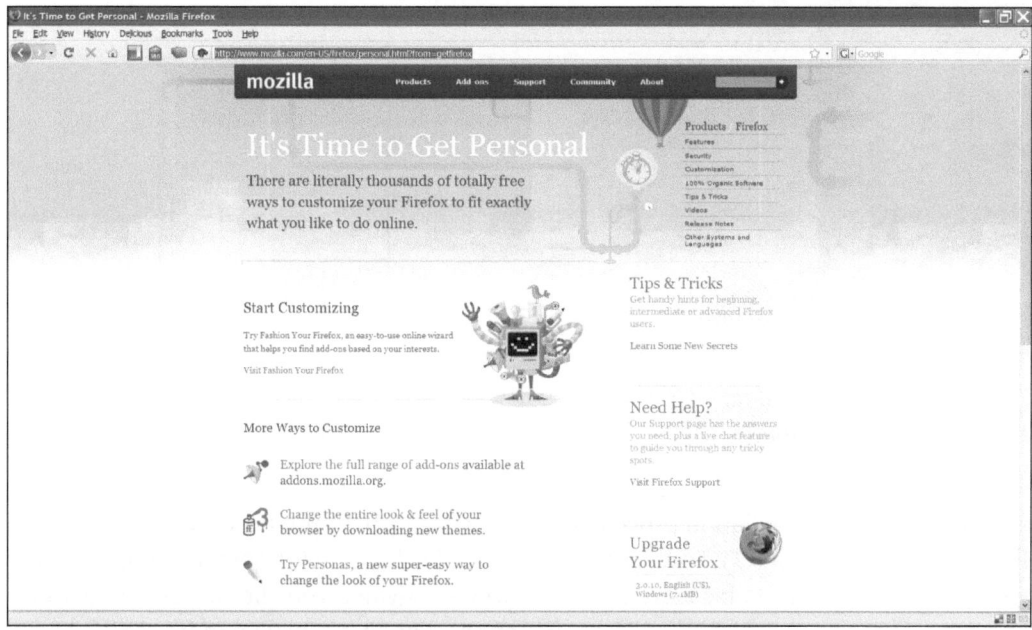

Figure 7-4. *The Firefox web browser home page as viewed on my 17" laptop screen*

Figure 7-5. *Firefox is available as a free download for your Windows netbook.*

Figure 7-6. *The Firefox Setup Wizard will guide you through the installation.*

Next, Firefox's installation process asks you to select between a Standard and Custom installation (see Figure 7-7). I recommend the Standard option for now. You might also wish to have Firefox installed as your default browser—when you click a web link (URL) in a document or email, Firefox will be the browser that opens instead of IE. (This will also allow you to save some hard drive space by uninstalling IE.) Uncheck this box if you wish to leave IE as the default browser. Click Next to continue.

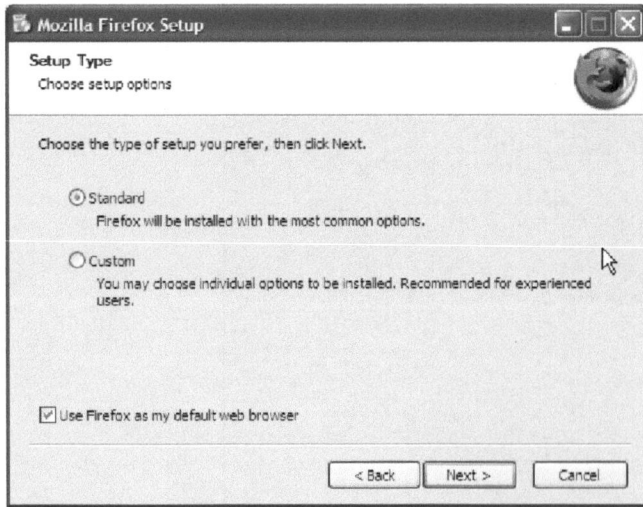

Figure 7-7. *Select the type of install and whether to have Firefox be your default browser.*

On the next screen (see Figure 7-8), you can see the directory where the Firefox application files are installed. (If you selected the Custom option shown in Figure 7-7, you can click the Browse button to choose a different location, which is useful if you like to install applications on a different hard drive or partition; however, most netbook users will want to leave the default location as it is). Click the Install button to continue.

The Setup wizard copies the files and installs Firefox. When the installation is complete, you will see a screen like the one in Figure 7-9. Click the Finish button to launch Firefox.

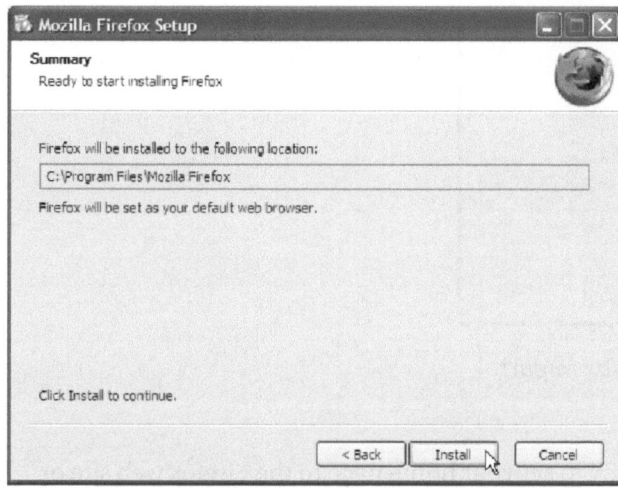

Figure 7-8. *Firefox will install in the Program Files directory by default.*

Figure 7-9. *The Firefox installation is complete and the browser is ready to use.*

The first time you run Firefox, you will see a screen like the one shown in Figure 7-10. Firefox is asking whether you wish to import your bookmarks, passwords, and browsing history from IE. Make your selection and click the Next button.

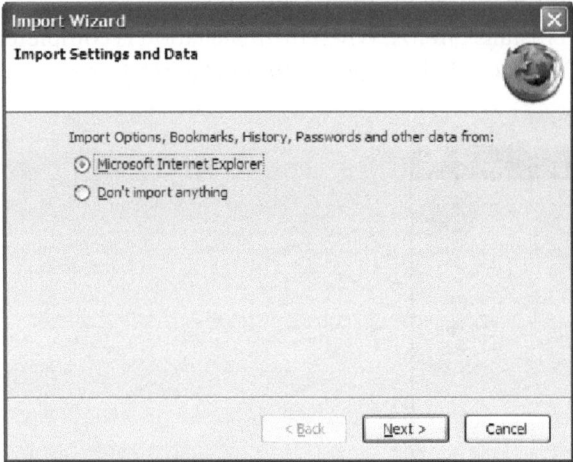

Figure 7-10. *You can choose to let Firefox import your settings from IE.*

You are also given the opportunity to set your home page to the Firefox web site or import the home page you've set in IE (see Figure 7-11). Make your selection and click Next. (I'll show you how to set your home page to something different, so don't worry if you don't like these choices.)

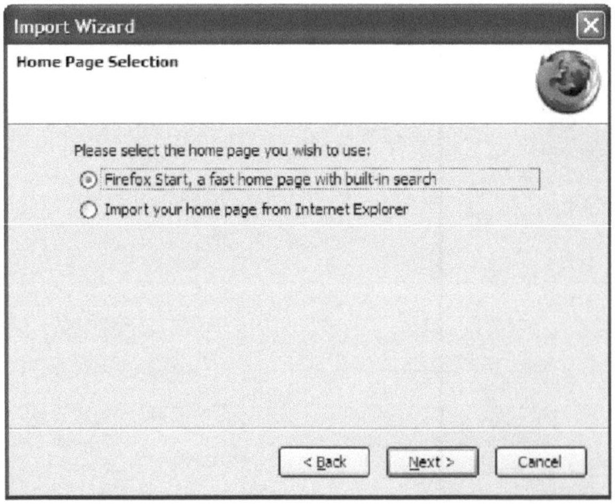

Figure 7-11. *Firefox will ask you to help it determine the home page that opens.*

If you elected for Firefox to import certain settings, these settings will be copied over to Firefox. Once it completes these tasks, Firefox will open up a browser window (see Figure 7-12); from here, you can find plenty of help and tutorials available that will teach you all about your new browser.

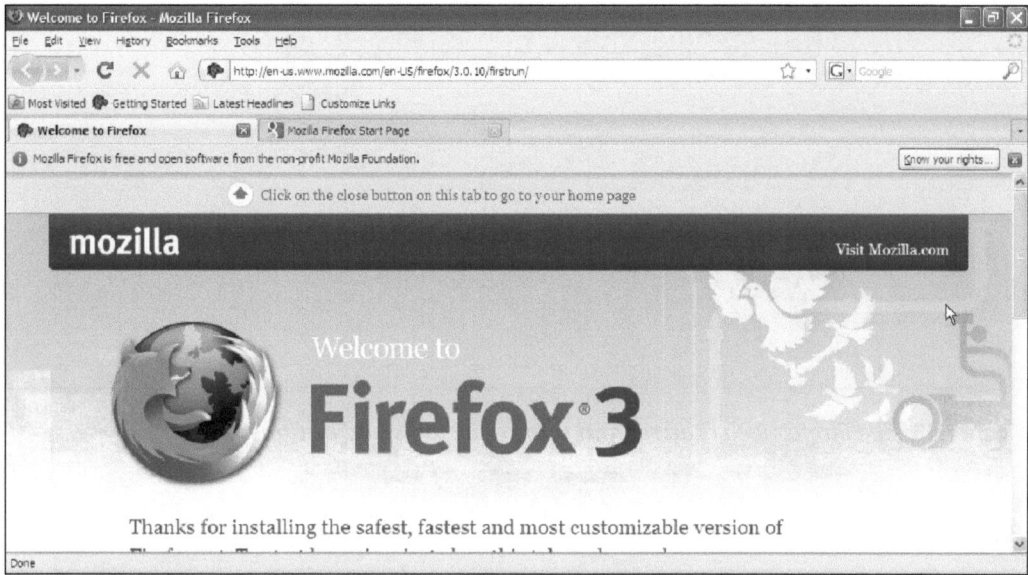

Figure 7-12. *Firefox provides you with tutorials for getting the most of the new browser.*

Firefox works like most browsers. It's got Back, Forward, Stop, and Home Page buttons (see Figure 7-13 for the location of many common features). You type in a web site you want to visit in the URL box at the top-center on the page, and you can perform a Google search without even visiting www.google.com by typing in what you wish to search in the Search toolbar in the upper-right corner. (Internet Explorer 7 and 8 allow you to specify the search engine that will provide results, so this isn't a feature that's unique to Firefox.)

I encourage you to view the tutorials, as well as click the Help menu and choose Help Contents; you'll find a FAQ, a search bar for typing in your question, and a link to the Knowledge Base and Forums where you can post questions, read responses, and get help from (and give help to) other Firefox users.

Figure 7-13. *The Firefox web browser and some of its tools and buttons*

Add-Ons

One Firefox features deserves special mention: add-ons. These are small mini-applications that run within the Firefox web browser. These mini-applications can perform all kinds of tasks, which can range from alerting you when you've received mail to providing instant weather reports. There are also add-ons for tracking packages you've sent or are expecting via UPS and FedEx, among others.

The best way to see how add-ons work is to visit the Firefox site and see what's available. Simply open Firefox, click the Tools menu, and then click the Add-ons option. A window will open like the one shown in Figure 7-14.

Now click the "Browse All Add-ons" link in the upper-right corner. Figure 7-15 shows the Firefox add-ons database that will open in your browser window.

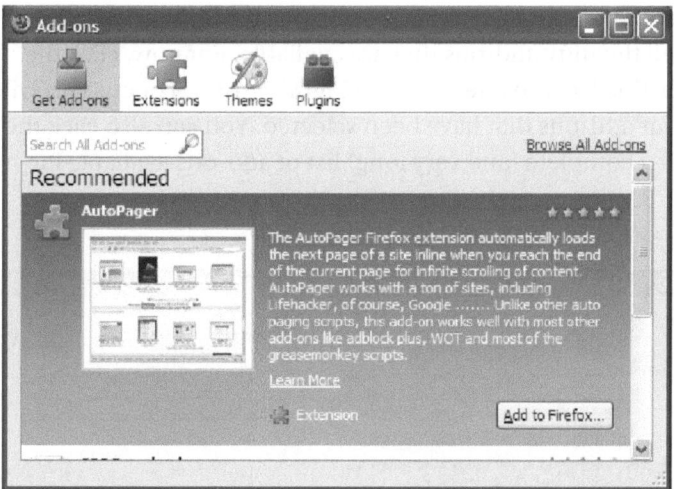

Figure 7-14. *You can manage your add-ons from this screen.*

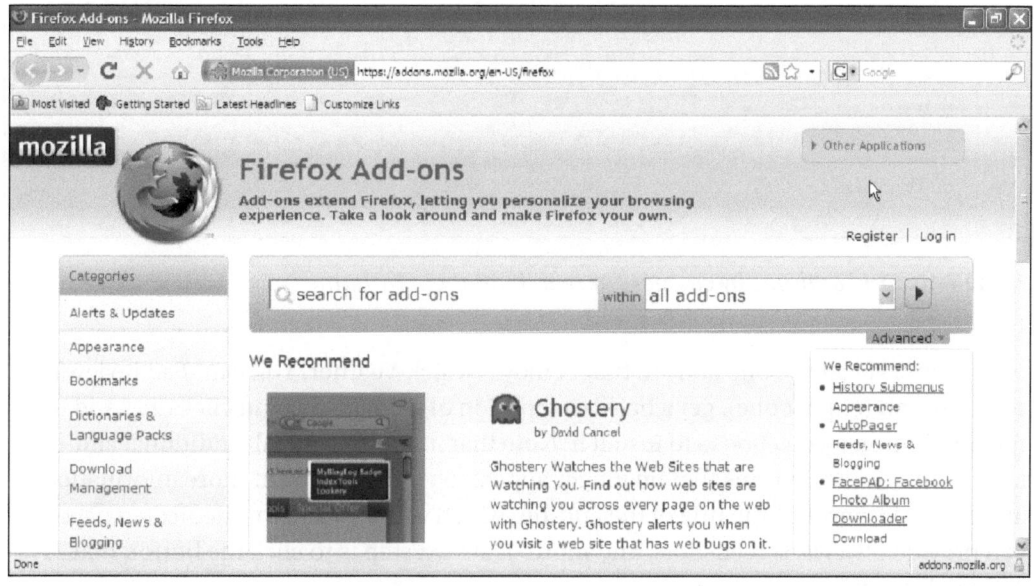

Figure 7-15. *You can spend hours searching the Firefox Add-ons database.*

Along the left edge of the screen is a list of categories. You should plan on spending some free time sifting through all the nifty add-ons that are available. For now, click the "Alerts & Updates" category; a listing like the one shown in Figure 7-16 will open. This will give you a list of the most popular add-ons that have been selected. You can also click the "See All Alerts & Updates" to get a complete (and very long) list of add-ons available for Firefox.

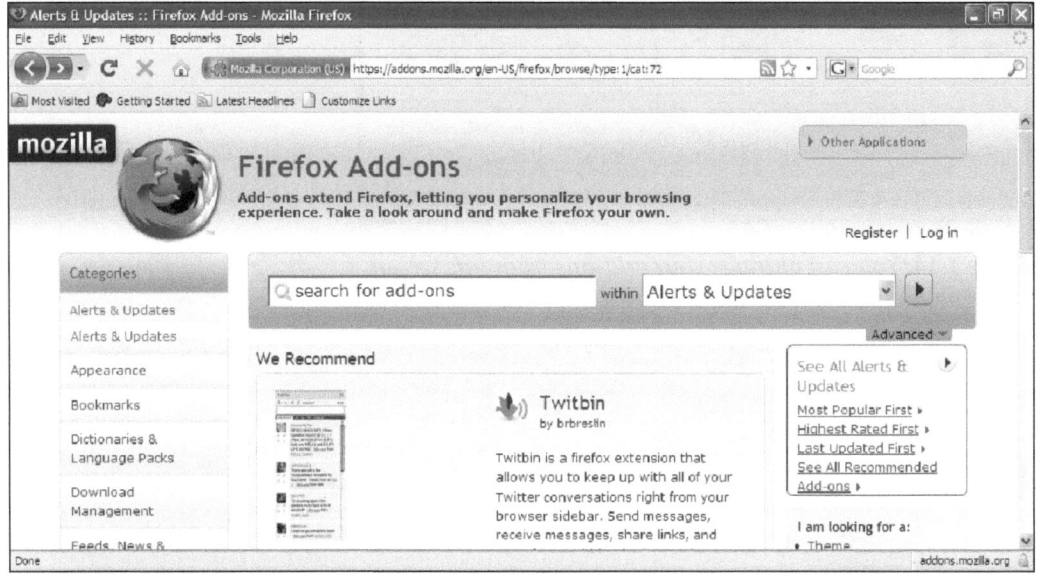

Figure 7-16. *Find add-ons by category or search for them by name*

Figure 7-17 shows one add-on that I enjoy: 1-ClickWeather. You can read reviews on every add-on (or post one), get a basic description of the add-on, and click the "Add to Firefox" button if you choose to install it. Note that it's easy to install additional add-ons later—or to delete add-ons that no longer appeal to you. If you want more information about an add-on, click the title of the add-on, which will take you to a dedicated page that can provide reviews, screenshots, and more. The next step is to click the button that says, "Add to Firefox."

A window will warn you that you should install add-ons only from authors you trust (see Figure 7-18); this add-on has more than 70,000 users and an average rating of 5 stars, so it looks trustworthy. All that's left is to click the Install Now button.

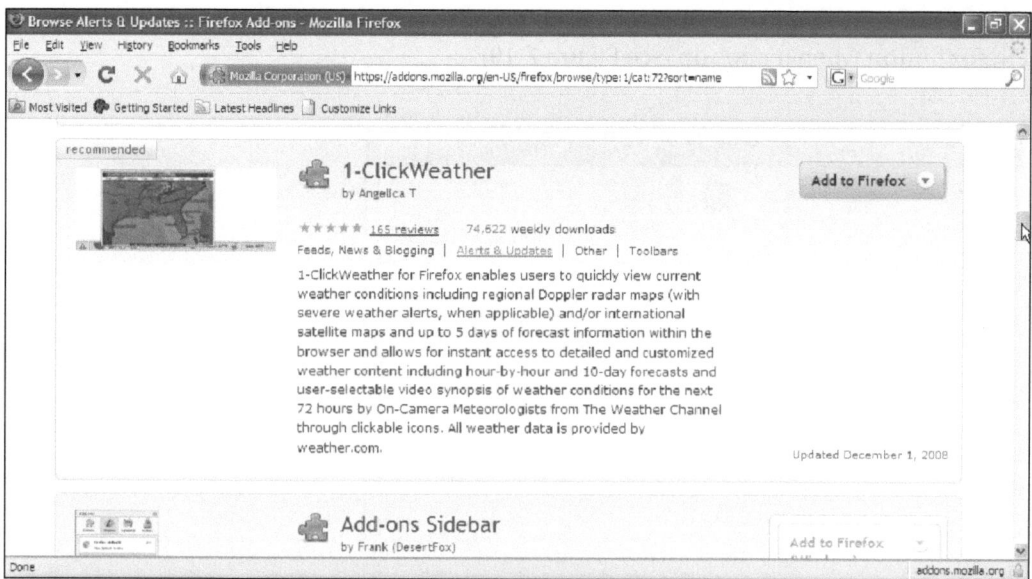

Figure 7-17. *1-ClickWeather looks like a promising add-on.*

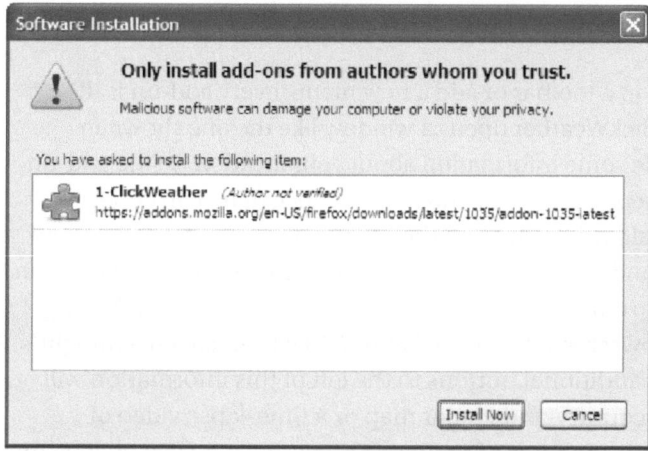

Figure 7-18. *You'll be warned about installing add-ons to your browser; proceed at your own risk.*

This add-on will install, and you will be asked to restart Firefox. Click the Restart Firefox button when it pops up (see Figure 7-19).

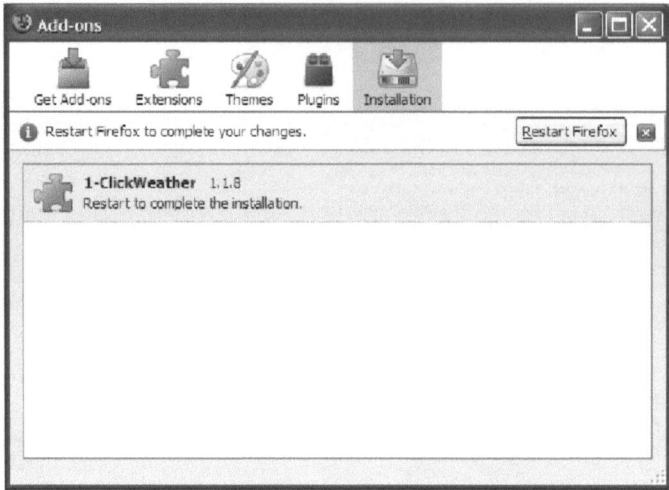

Figure 7-19. *After installing an add-on, you need to restart Firefox to use it.*

Some add-ons place a button on a toolbar or add a new menu; every add-on is different. After restarting Firefox, 1-ClickWeather opens a window like the one shown in Figure 7-20; you're asked to provide some information about your location, so the add-on can provide you with the correct weather forecast and maps. Notice that I can choose where to have the information displayed (such as on the Menu Bar or the Status Bar), and I can choose between Fahrenheit and Celsius values. Next, I click on the Save & Exit button.

At this point, I can now see the current temperature (77 degrees Fahrenheit) along the bottom edge of my Firefox browser window (see Figure 7-21); I can also see tonight's low and tomorrow's forecast. The additional buttons to the left of this information will open various windows showing a country-wide radar map or a time-lapse video of weather patterns, among other weather items of interest. Remember, you can change the location of 1-ClickWeather information by moving your mouse's pointer over the displayed information and right-clicking. This brings up the setup window, where you can make any changes you like.

To remove an add-on, click the Tools menu, select Add-ons, and click the Extensions tab in the window that appears. All the add-ons you have installed will be listed. Click the Disable to temporarily turn an Add-on off or click the Uninstall button to remove it. You'll have to restart Firefox for the Uninstall option to take effect.

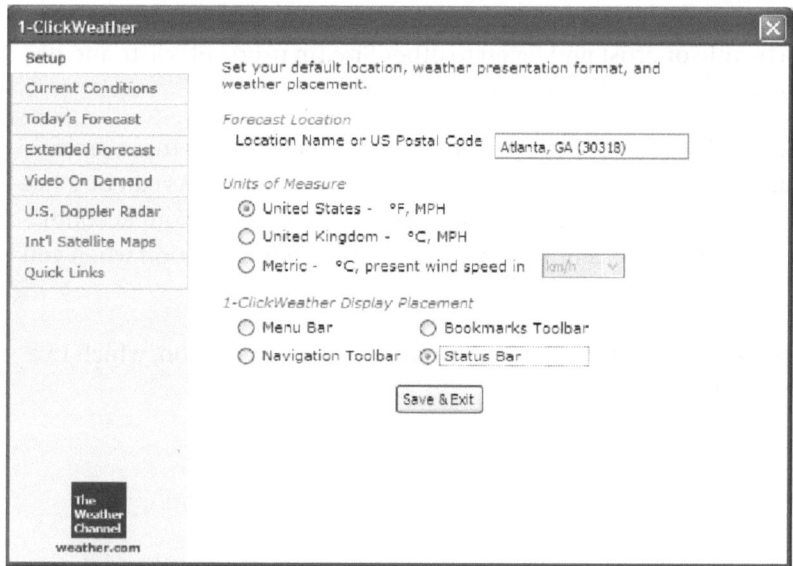

Figure 7-20. *1-ClickWeather asks for some basic information*

Figure 7-21. *1-ClickWeather now gives me my local weather in my web browser.*

I have no doubt that you'll find one or more extremely useful add-ons to add to your Firefox browser. But just in case you're overwhelmed with options, let me offer up a few suggestions before I close out this discussion on Firefox:

Download Web Videos. If you find an occasional YouTube (www.youtube.com) video you'd like to download and share with others (maybe when you're not connected to the Internet), `Video Download Helper` is a nice add-on. Download the video to your hard drive and watch these videos even when you're not online.

Organize your Favorite Bookmarks. Stop searching for that needle-in-a-haystack web site you bookmarked years ago. Use the `Delicious Bookmarks` add-on and every time you add a favorite web site to your bookmarks, tag it with some keywords that you can use to later search through and filter all your bookmarks.

Listen to Online Music. Search for music you like and then listen to it using the `Fire.fm` add-on. Search by title or artist and listen to other Fire.fm users' playlists and discover new music categories you might have missed.

Keep Passwords Secure. If you're online, you've probably got accounts that require a username and password. Keeping track of all these different accounts can be a hassle, so let `LastPass Password Manager` add-on do it for you. It will keep your account info secure and encrypted, but easily allow you to enter login information when you need it.

To find any of these items, simply search on the name of a given add-on, which I've provided, in quotation marks.

Chrome

Before I end this chapter, I'd like to let you know about a new web browser that's slowly but surely making waves. It's called Chrome, and it's from a company you might have heard of in the news: Google. Yes, Google, the king of search engines, has gotten into the web browser business. Chrome is free to download by visiting `http://chrome.google.com` and clicking the big "Download Google Chrome" button you see in Figure 7-22.

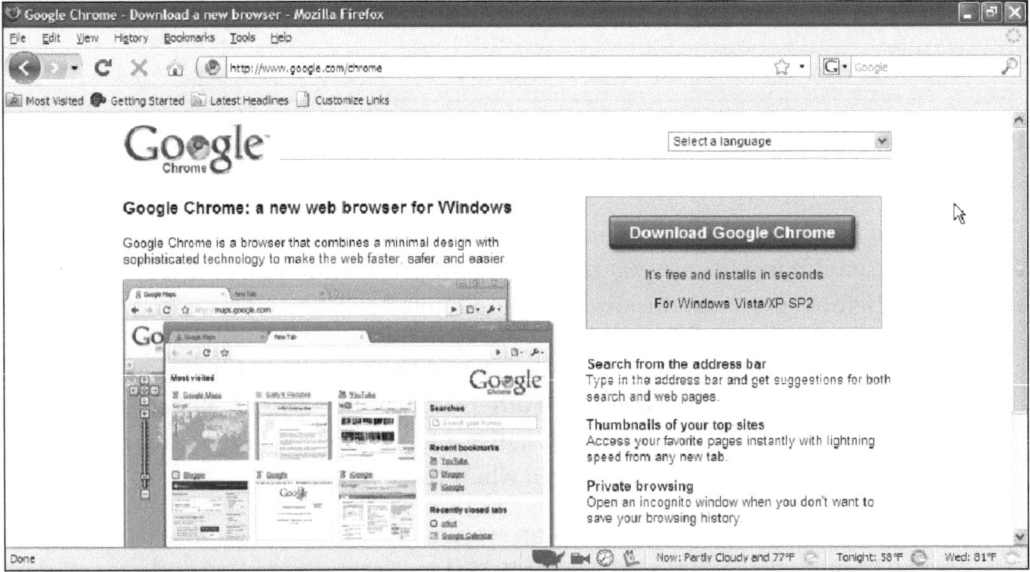

Figure 7-22. *Google Chrome is a new web browser available as a free download.*

Chrome is what I would call a no-frills browser. There are not a lot of features, but this is often what many Internet users want: a screen that's simple and uncluttered. If that's what you're looking for, then you'll probably enjoy Chrome. I can't give up my Firefox Add-ons, but once Chrome is upgraded to support them (and Google is well-known for tinkering with and improving its free applications), I might have to give it a second look.

What's Next?

Besides using your web browser to visit web sites, you'll find there are a lot more things you can do with your browser. For example, two of my favorite and most-used applications aren't even installed on my netbook; they're cloud computing applications (refer back to Chapter 4 for a discussion on cloud computing), and I use my Firefox web browser to gain access to them. If you're not already familiar with them, I can't wait to introduce you to Google Mail (Gmail) and Google Calendar.

CHAPTER 8

###

Netbook Email

In the previous chapter, I introduced you to Firefox, a great web browser that I use instead of Microsoft Internet Explorer. But there are other free web browsers out there, including Chrome, Opera, and Safari. There is ongoing debate as to which web browser is the best, but one thing is certain: you'll need a good web browser to enjoy all the new applications that are being developed specifically for use with web browsers.

In Chapter 4, I introduced the topic of cloud computing, where, rather than installing an application on your netbook, you instead point your web browser at a web address. The application you'll be using runs on a far-away computer (also known as a server) and will often require you to log in with a username and password to use the program. A good example of this is online banking, where you can log in to transfer funds from savings to checking. YouTube.com is another good cloud computing example. This site lets you upload videos and even do some rudimentary editing. Finally, there's Facebook (`www.facebook.com`), which allows you to connect with friends and family. These online applications are always running and always available, as long as you have an active Internet connection. Your browser makes the connection, and you enjoy whatever services are available with the online application.

Google offers some of today's most popular cloud computing applications at absolutely no cost to you. Google Sites (`sites.google.com`) offers a service where you can create your own web site for free. Google Maps (`maps.google.com`) lets you get directions and plan routes from A to B, as well as view street and satellite images of your destinations—again, at no cost. Chapter 5 already covered Google Docs, which includes word processor, spreadsheet, and slideshow applications that you access from your web browser.

I probably sound like a Google Super Fan, and I am! Google has jumped on the cloud computing bus in a big way, and it continues to release new (and free) applications fairly frequently. And while I always enjoy learning and playing around with Google's latest toys—er, tools—I have yet to find anything I rely on more than two of the company's oldest and most popular applications: Google Mail and Google Calendar. Each of these feature-packed applications warrants its own chapter. I'll cover Google Mail in this chapter and Google Calendar in Chapter 9.

Google Mail

If you have not already created a Google account, refer back to Chapter 5 for instructions on creating one. Once you set up an account, visit www.gmail.com and log in with your username and password. The first time Google Mail (Gmail) opens, you'll see a screen like the one shown in Figure 8-1.

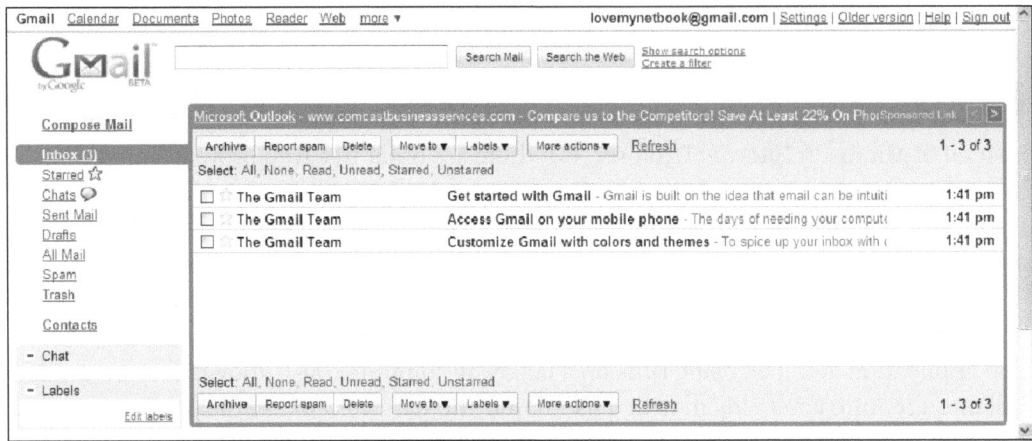

Figure 8-1. *Gmail's simple user interface is easy to learn and use.*

Let's examine a few areas of the screen in greater detail, so you'll have a better understanding of how Gmail works. First, take a look at the left side of Figure 8-1, which shows the equivalent of Gmail's folders: Inbox, Starred, Chats, Sent Mail, Drafts, All Mail, Spam, and Trash. In Gmail, incoming messages are sent to the Inbox by default; Figure 8-1 also shows that I've received three messages from The Gmail Team, welcoming me to Gmail. To open an email and read it, click it—the message opens as shown in Figure 8-2.

If you've ever wondered how Google can possibly make Gmail free to use, here's your answer: look along the right edge of an opened email message, and you'll see a few advertisements. These ads are paid for by companies that want to get your attention and hope you'll buy what they're selling. The advertisements are also typically selected based on keywords found in your email message. If you get an email from a friend asking about Tuesday night's Atlanta Braves baseball game, you're likely to see three or four advertisements for Braves' caps, shirts, autographs, and other sport memorabilia. Gmail scans the incoming message for keywords and tries to find advertisements that might be relevant.

After reading an email, you have the same options you'll find in most email applications (such as Microsoft Outlook). Figure 8-3 displays some of the available options and how to access them.

Figure 8-2. *Clicking an email message opens it for reading, replying, and other options.*

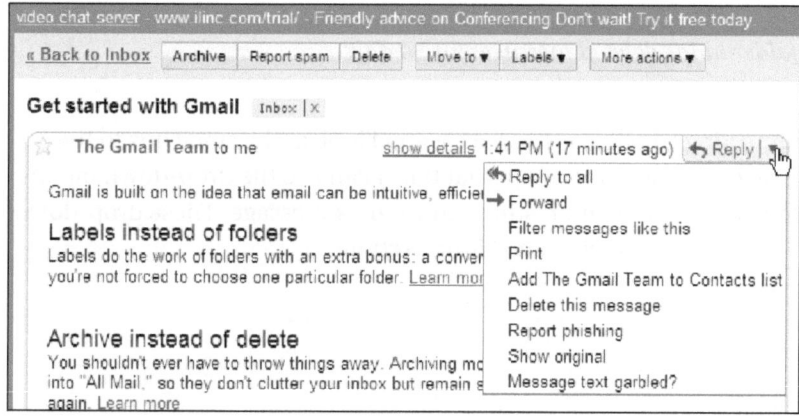

Figure 8-3. *You can delete, reply, or forward an email and much more.*

Clicking the Archive button sends a message to the All Mail folder. Think of this as an archive where emails are safe until you delete them. Google currently gives you more than 7GB (gigabytes) of storage space, and it increases the storage limit regularly, so expect this capacity to go up over time. (There are Gmail users who never delete any email; they can go back years and find any email using Gmail's built-in search feature.)

The Report Spam button sends the message to the Spam folder and future messages from that sender will go immediately to the Spam folder. The Delete button sends the message to the Trash folder—after 30 days, the message will be deleted automatically, unless you move the message to another folder. Clicking the Reply drop-down as shown in Figure 8-4 gives you more options, such as the ability to reply to all, filter your email, add the sender to your Contacts list, and many other abilities.

If I click the Delete button, Google Mail sends the message to the Trash folder. If I click the Trash folder, I can see the message I just deleted (see Figure 8-4).

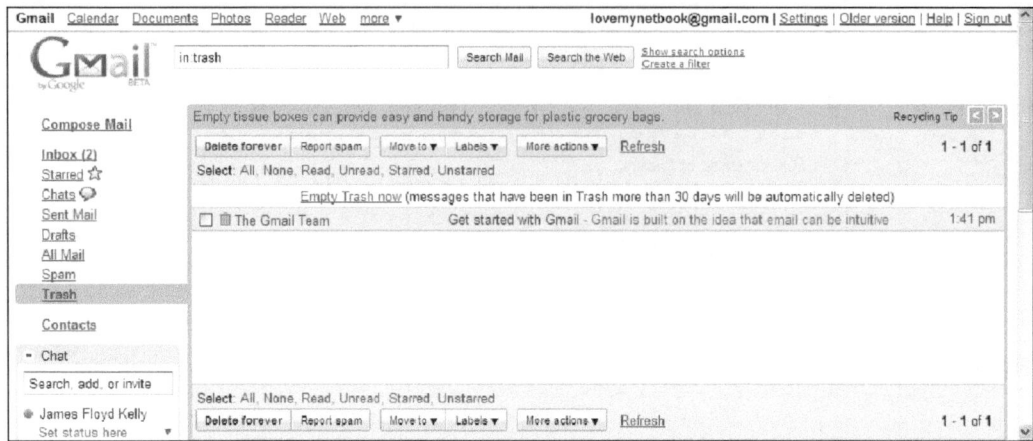

Figure 8-4. *The Trash folder holds deleted messages for 30 days.*

Now, here's an interesting Gmail feature. Take a good look at the small box to the left of the deleted message. If I place a check in that box, I can use the drop-down menus shown in Figure 8-5 to perform more interesting actions on a message. These drop-down messages are labeled "Move to," "Labels," and "More Actions."

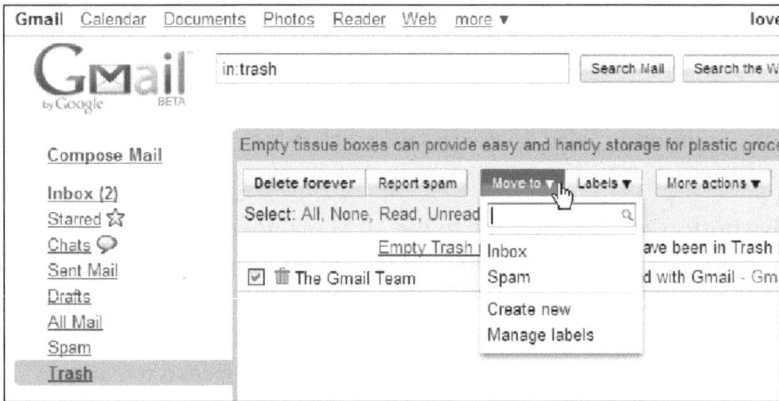

Figure 8-5. *Place a check in a message's box to gain access to even more features.*

In Figure 8-5, I've clicked the "Move to" drop-down box, and I can now choose to send this message to the Inbox or Spam folders. In Figure 8-6, I've clicked the "More Actions" drop-down box, and I can now mark the message as unread or filter similar messages.

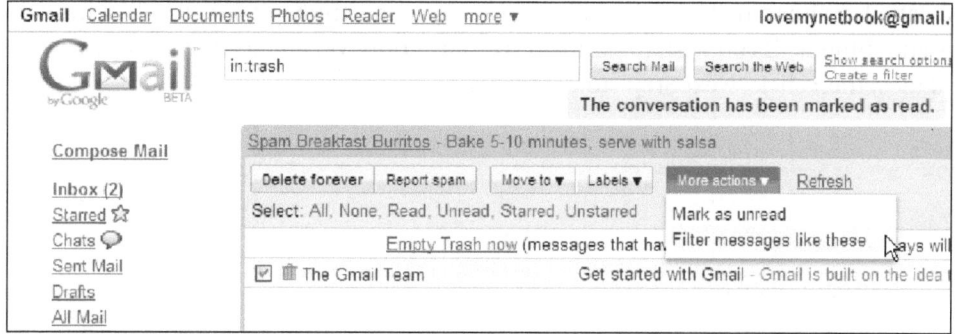

Figure 8-6. *I can return a message to Unread status or filter future messages like it.*

You might wonder what filtering is all about. When an email comes in, it typically goes straight to your Inbox. But let's say you get a variety of emails from friends, family, and co-workers, so many that you'd prefer never to have to deal with any more messages from The Gmail Team. Gmail will let you perform actions such as Mark as Read or Delete the second an email arrives; executed properly, these actions can ensure you never even see a given email. Here's how it works.

Begin by placing a check in the box to the left of a message you wish to filter (see Figure 8-7). You can choose to filter the message by examining the sender's name or even certain words in the Subject line of the message. For example, assume you want to delete email from The Gmail Team automatically. Click "More actions" and then select "Filter messages like these."

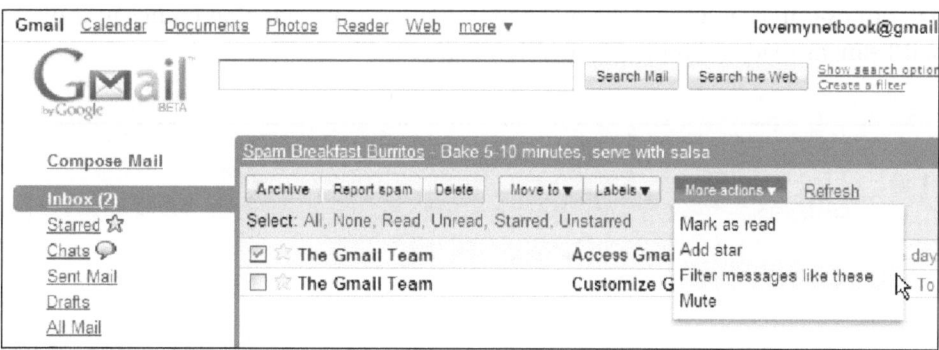

Figure 8-7. *The Select box enables you to filter messages from The Gmail Team.*

A screen appears like the one shown in Figure 8-8. Note that you can filter messages based on who sent a message (such as The Gmail Team), who received the message, or on specific text that appears in the message's subject line. You can filter on certain words that appear in the text of the message, or even on words that do *not* appear!

You can also filter emails that include an attachment; simply place a check in the box for "Has attachment" if you wish to perform special actions on emails that arrive with attached files, then click "Next Step" to continue.

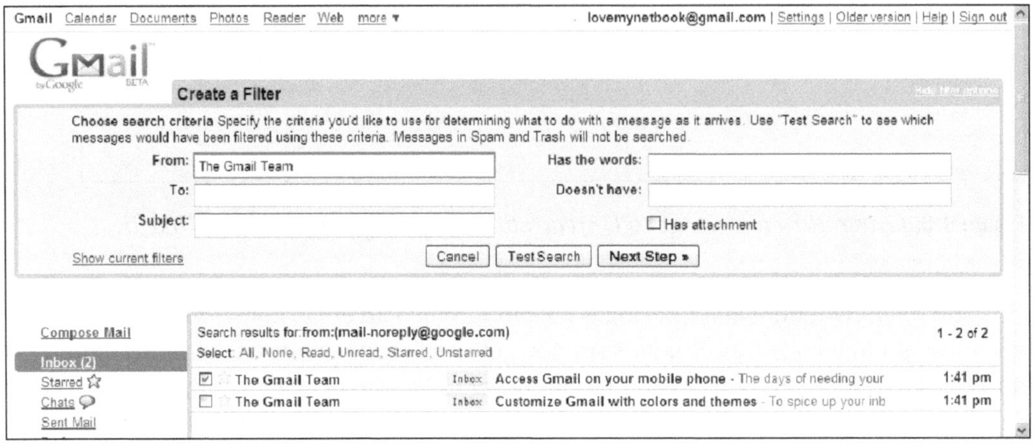

Figure 8-8. *You can choose to let Firefox import your settings from Internet Explorer.*

The next screen (see Figure 8-9) lets you choose what to do to the filtered emails. Options include sending the email straight to All Mail (archiving it), marking the message as read and applying a label to it (I'll explain labels momentarily), forwarding or deleting the message, and much more. You can also choose multiple actions on a given email, such as marking an email as read, forwarding it to a different email account, and then deleting it. For example, assume that you want to mark every email that comes in from The Gmail Team as read and then delete it (see Figure 8-9).

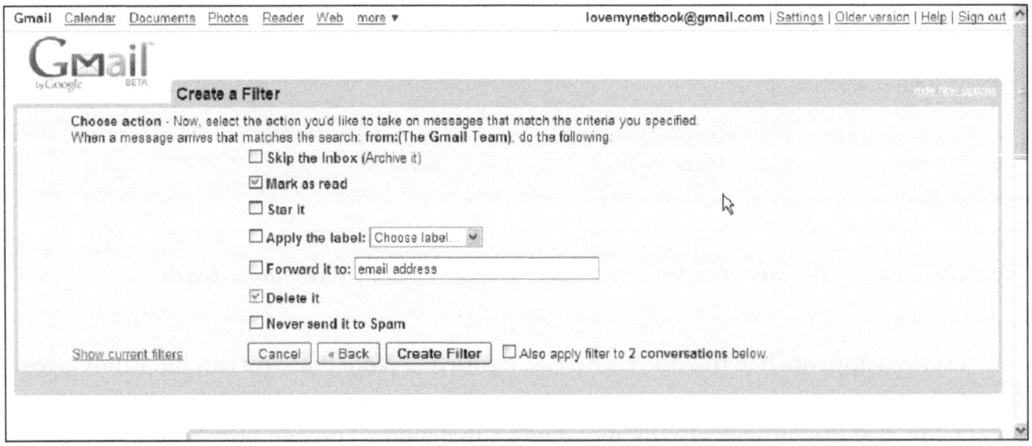

Figure 8-9. *Firefox will ask you to help it determine the home page that opens.*

Click the "Create Filter" button to start the filtering process. (You can also place a check in the box labeled "Also apply filter to X conversations below." This applies the filter to your entire Inbox, even covering messages that have already been received prior to the creation of the filter—nice!) Figure 8-10 shows the new filter (and any other existing filters)—you can click the edit link to modify it or the delete link to remove it.

Figure 8-10. *View and manage your filters from the Filters tab.*

Note that Figure 8-10 shows the Filters tab of the Settings screen. You can click the Settings link in the upper-right corner of the screen to access this tab and others, including: General, Accounts, Labels, Forwarding and POP/IMAP, Chat, Web Clips, Labs, and Themes. I won't cover all of these tabs, but I encourage you to click them all and look them over—most of them are fairly self-explanatory. If you need additional help with a tab, click the Help link in the upper-right corner, and you'll find all the answers you need on Gmail's online database of questions and answers. In the meantime, click the Labels tab (see Figure 8-11) to discover another nice feature of Gmail.

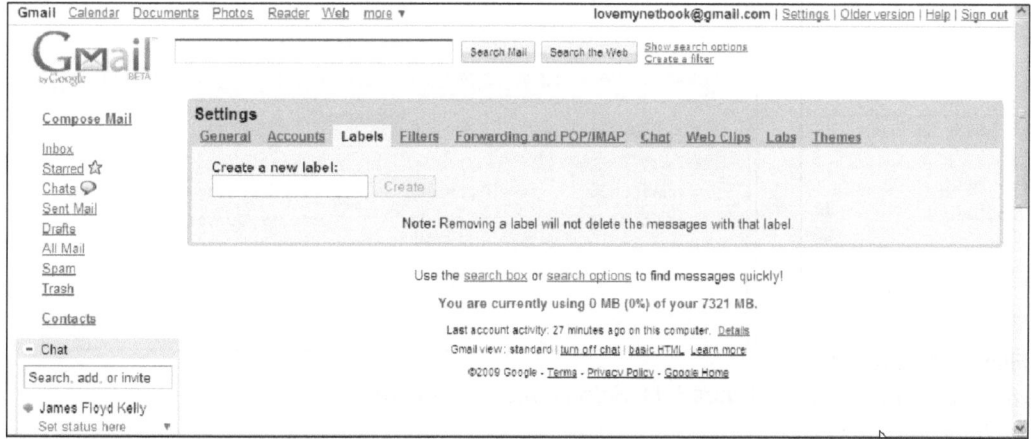

Figure 8-11. *The Labels feature is a powerful tool you're going to love.*

I'll walk you through how to use the Labels feature by showing you how I use it, changing only the names and email addresses of my contacts (for obvious reasons). I begin by creating a new label called Urgent in the "Create a new label" text box (see Figure 8-11) and then clicking the Create button. Now I create two more labels: Low and Apress (see Figure 8-12 for a list of my labels).

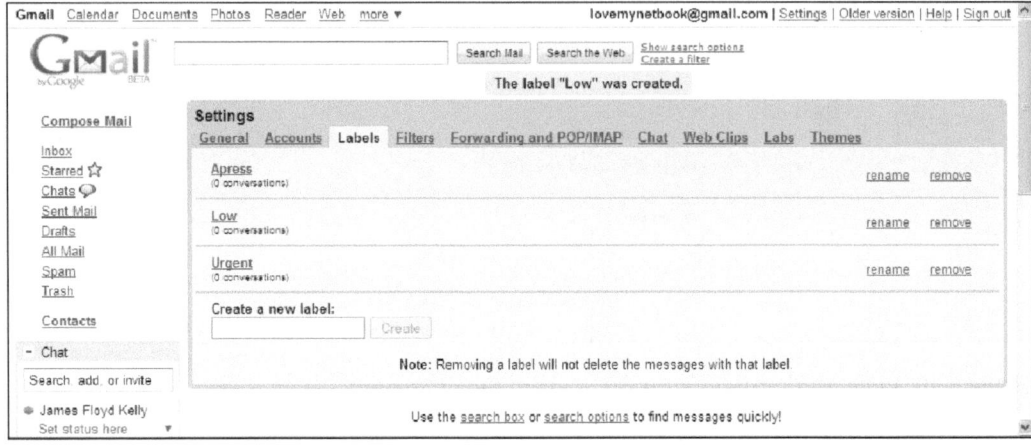

Figure 8-12. *I created labels to apply to my email messages.*

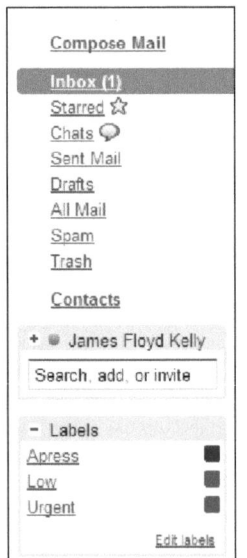

Next, I click the Inbox. Note how there is a section for Labels beneath the list of folders (see Figure 8-13). I click the small box to the right of each label to select a color for that label.

Now I'm ready to assign a filter to an email. Figure 8-14 shows a few messages in my Inbox; I place a check in one message's Select box and click the Labels drop-down list to assign the Apress label to the selected message.

Figure 8-13. *Labels applied to an email include both text and color.*

Figure 8-14. *Select a message to add a label.*

Figure 8-15 shows that message with the bright blue Apress label attached (trust me—it's blue).

Figure 8-15. *A message's label makes it easier to find in a long list of emails.*

I can go back and create a filter that adds the Apress label to any emails that come from the people at my publisher—all messages sent from peterrabbit@ apress.com, paulbunyan@apress.com, and maryquitecontrary@apress.com immediately acquire the Apress label when they arrive in my Inbox.

By the way—you can assign multiple labels to a single email. One of my favorite things about labels is the ability to view all messages, even those in the All Mail archive folder, by clicking a label's name in the Label box (see Figure 8-13). It's a great way to filter all your emails. If you create a nice selection of labels and then create some useful filters, you can get a firm grasp on email management. I have about eight labels and 20 filters—I use them to sort my messages from my publisher, my family, and even newsletters (see Figure 8-16). Rarely do I ever get an email that doesn't have some sort of label applied.

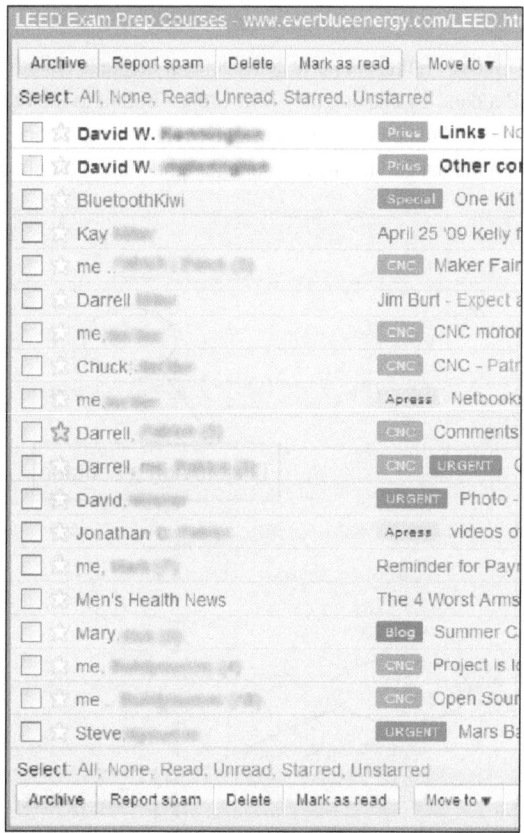

Figure 8-16. *Labels are a powerful feature I take maximum advantage of.*

More Gmail Features

Gmail is always adding new features; it places "New Features" announcements in the upper-right corner when there is something new to show you. Let's take a quick look at a couple more fun things you can do to improve your email experience a little better.

Contacts List

In addition to holding the email addresses of your friends, family members, and co-workers, the contact list lets you store information such as address, birthday, and phone numbers (see Figure 8-17). Click the "Contacts" link seen in this Figure, and you can add new contacts, sort existing ones, and more. Click a contact's name to view that contact's information and add or make changes.

Note Gmail supports collections of contacts called Groups. For example, create a group called "Golfing Buddies" by clicking the "New Group" button to the right of the "New Contact" button (see Figure 8-17) and add the email addresses of all your golfing friends. The next time you need to email all of them about a potential game day, just send an email to the group name instead of typing in all their email addresses!

Figure 8-17. *You'll find contact information such as phone and email in the Contacts list.*

Chat

Gmail has a built-in chat tool (also called instant messaging, or IM). You can see how it works in Figure 8-18; simply expand the Chat link and move your mouse pointer over a contact to bring up a small window. Click this window's Chat button to initiate a chat with the selected contact.

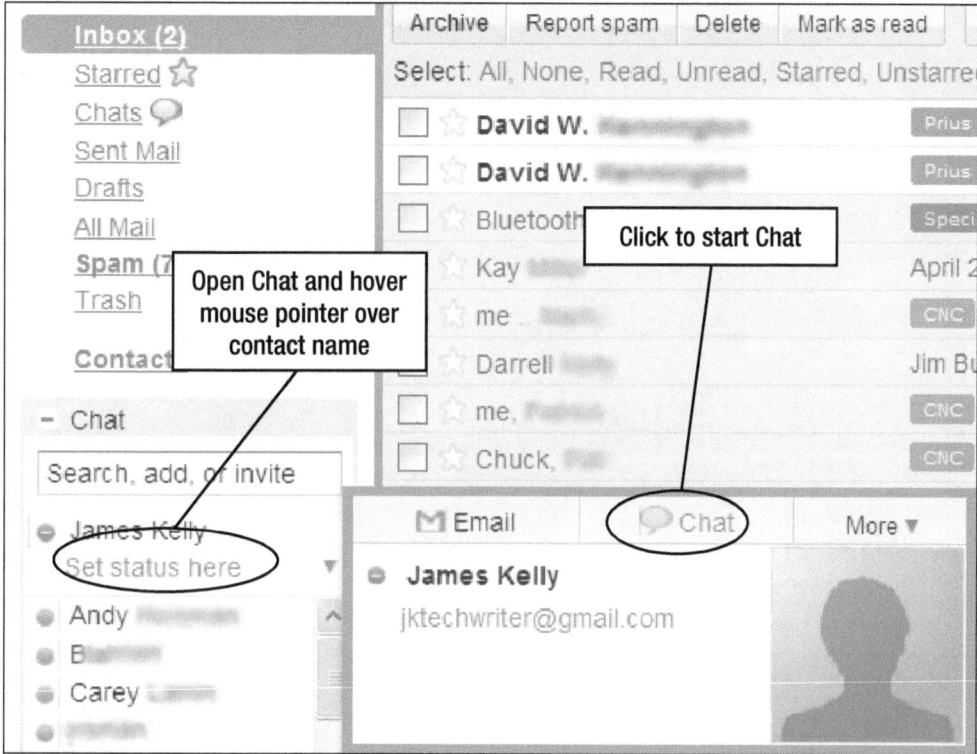

Figure 8-18. *Chat live with a contact using the Chat feature.*

A box will open like the one shown in Figure 8-19. Type your message in the box and hit the Enter key. If your contact is online and willing to participate, your contact's replies will appear in the same box.

Figure 8-19. *The Chat window lets you communicate with another Gmail user.*

What's Next

If you're impressed with Gmail, you're probably going to love Google Calendar, which I'll cover in Chapter 9. In fact, the two applications work very well together and can make your life much easier. Google Calendar is free to use, and you might find, as I have, that it can quickly become an indispensable tool for both personal and work-related activities.

CHAPTER 9

■■■

Netbook Calendar

In Chapter 8 I introduced you to Gmail and many of its best features. Because it's an online application, your email is always available when you're online, and not just from your netbook. You can login to Gmail from any Internet-connected computer, making Gmail a truly portable email application.

In this chapter, I want to introduce you to what I consider to be Gmail's sidekick (or maybe it's the other way around)—Google Calendar. This online application is also available to you from any computer that's connected to the Internet. Google Calendar is the perfect organizer/planner for your netbook, too; it's lightweight (there's no software to install in terms of storage space) and extremely fast when navigating around days, months, and years. Entering events into your Google Calendar is also extremely simple— you have two methods to choose from when adding appointments and three methods for getting reminders! (Google Calendar has saved me more than once from missing an important appointment because I use its ability to send text message reminders to my mobile phone; I'll show you how that works later in this chapter.)

For me, Google Calendar is one of the best examples of a cloud computing application done well. It's free to use, has an uncluttered interface, and works with any browser, even the one on your mobile phone if you have that feature. Add in the ability to "publish" your calendar (or a public calendar you can create) and allow others to view it, and maybe you're starting to get an idea of its power. But enough of the sales pitch: Let me walk you through how great and easy-to-use Google Calendar really is.

Google Calendar

If you haven't already created a Google Account, refer back to Chapter 5 for instructions on creating one. Once you set up an account, visit http://calendar.google.com and login with your username and password (see Figure 9-1).

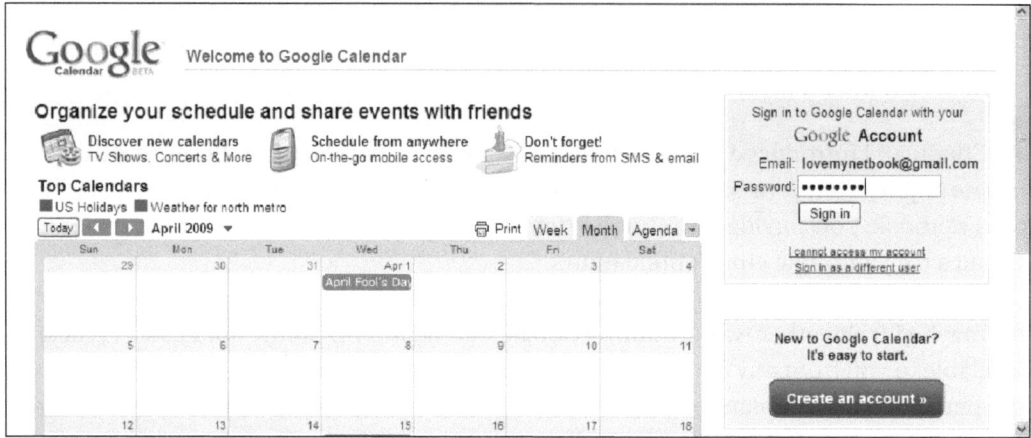

Figure 9-1. *Google Calendar is a free-to-use application that requires a Google user account.*

You'll be asked to provide some information the first time you log in to Google Calendar (see Figure 9-2). The information you supply enables Google Calendar to configure the calendar with your proper time zone. Click the Continue button after you supply the information.

Google Calendar opens as shown in Figure 9-3. The first thing you need to know is that the calendar displays in Week view by default. This means a week's worth of appointments are displayed in column format by one-hour increments. You can see that there are five views in Figure 9-3: Day, Week, Month, 4 Days, and Agenda. These are tabs in the upper-right corner of the screen. You can click a tab to select a view or press a shortcut key on the keyboard. You'll find that Calendar has plenty of shortcut keys.

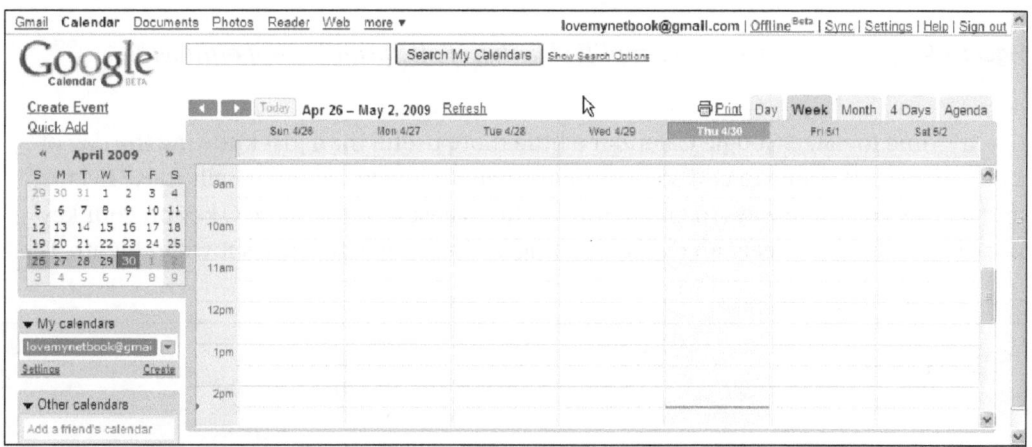

Welcome to Google Calendar

Welcome back, James Floyd. Before using Google Calendar, we need to know a little more about you. Please enter the add

If you want to use the Google Calendar service as part of a separate Google Account, click here. (Note: you can only be log Account at a time)

Get started with Google Calendar

First name: James Floyd

Last name: Kelly

Location: United States

Time zone: (GMT-05:00) Eastern Time
☐ Display all timezones

Continue

Figure 9-2. *Supply your location and time zone to start using Google Calendar.*

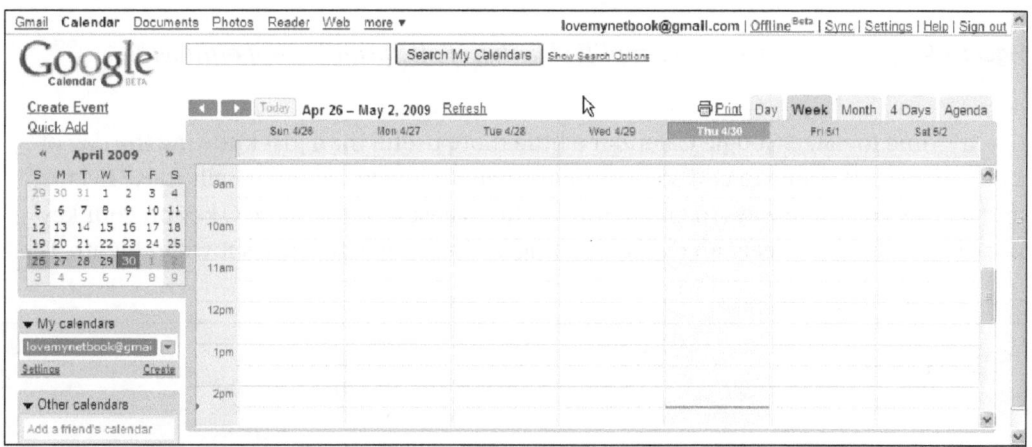

Figure 9-3. *Google Calendar opens in Week mode, but you can change this easily.*

Press the M key. Notice that this changes the calendar to Month view and gives the screen a standard calendar look. Press the D key to change to Day view, which displays an entire day's worth of appointments. Press A for Agenda view which lists upcoming appointments in an easy-to-view, non-graphical format as shown in Figure 9-4. The 4 Days view requires a mouse click, unfortunately. I prefer the Monthly view, so the remaining screenshots in this chapter use that format unless otherwise specified.

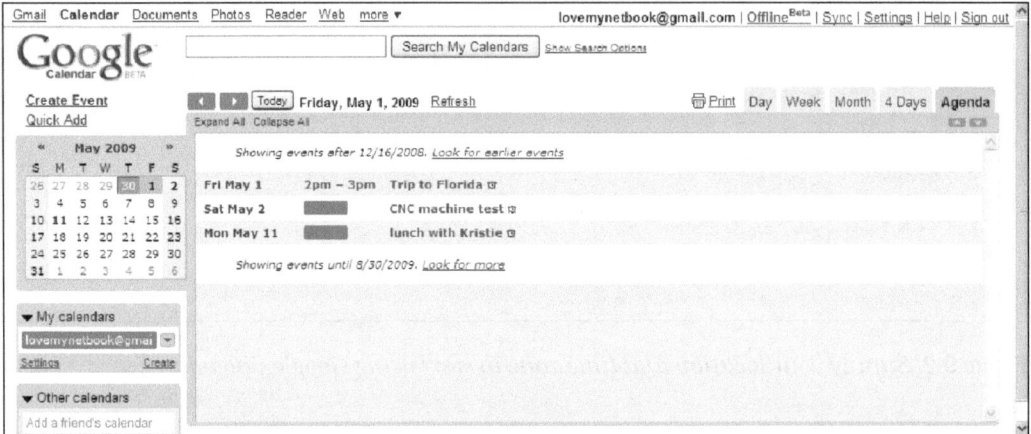

Figure 9-4. *Agenda mode offers a simplified listing of all upcoming appointments.*

It's time to make Google Calendar a little more useful than just knowing the day of a certain date. It's time to add some appointments. Google Calendar calls these Events, and it gives you three ways to create them. The easiest is to press the C key on your keyboard. This lets you create an event, opening a window like the one shown in Figure 9-5.

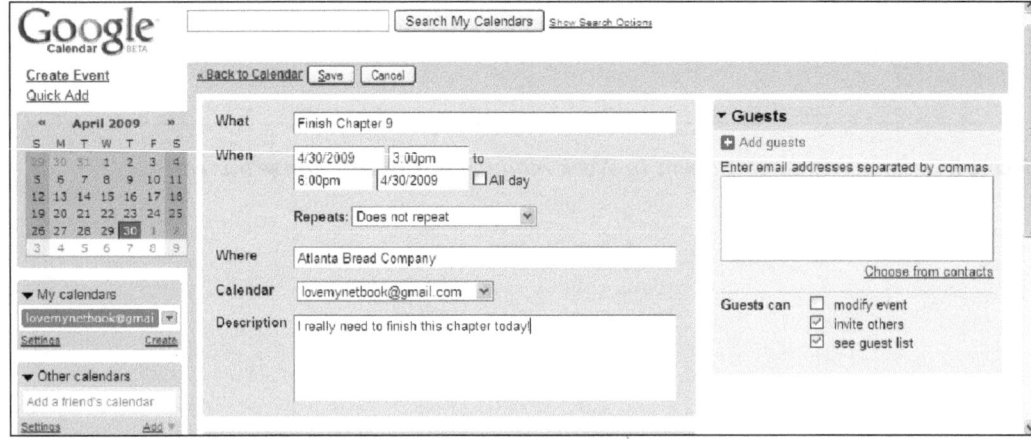

Figure 9-5. *Creating an event is as easy as pressing the C key on your keyboard.*

In Figure 9-5, I've entered some information into some of the fields. I gave my event a name ("Finish Chapter 9"), and I specified the start and end times (3 p.m. and 6 p.m., respectively). I also provided a location (Atlanta Bread Company) and a note to myself in the Description text box. (Don't worry about all the other stuff you see on this page; I'll cover the rest of it a bit later.)

When I'm done, I click the Save button just above the "What" box where you type the name of your event. This adds the event to my calendar (see Figure 9-6).

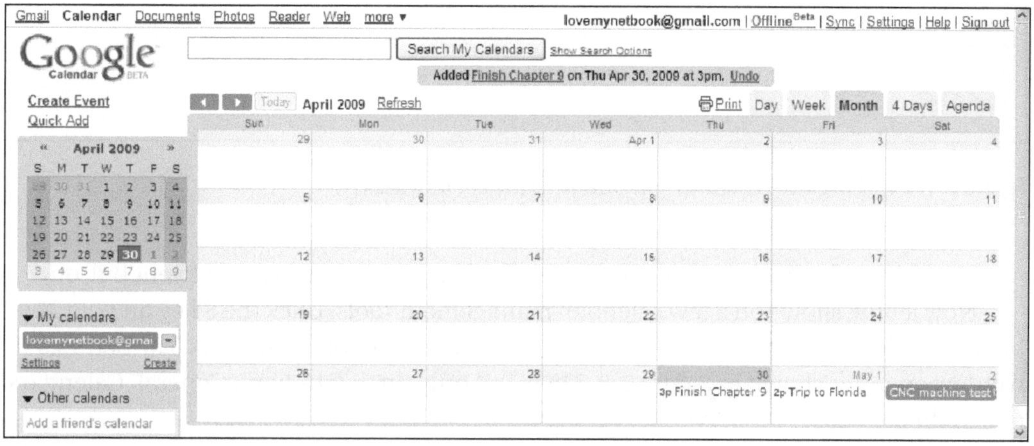

Figure 9-6. *My event has been added to my calendar.*

I mentioned earlier that there are three ways to add events. The second method is to click the "Create Event" link in the upper-left corner of the screen (just below the Google Calendar logo). This opens up the same event-creation window that you saw in Figure 9-5. The third method is to click the date (or time) in the calendar portion of the screen, which brings up a bubble window (see Figure 9-7). Enter the name of your event and click the "Create Event" button.

Note If you click a day while in Month view, Google Calendar schedules an all-day event. If you click a specific time (in Day or Week view), Google Calendar specifies the time of the event on the calendar. Click the "Edit event details" link in the bubble window if you wish to add a description, location, or modify the time. Then click the Create Event button to add the event.

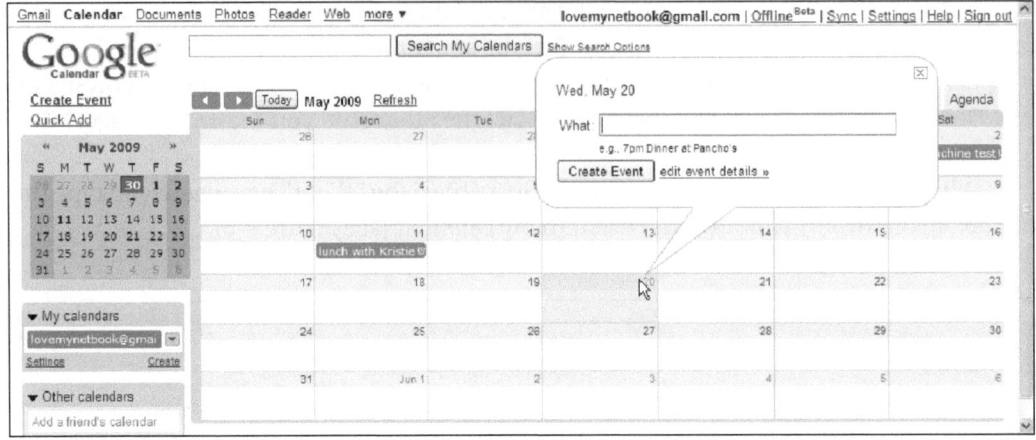

Figure 9-7. *Clicking the calendar lets you add an event quickly.*

Your event should be visible on the screen after you click the Create Event button.

Now let me show you a few calendar-management tools. Click the S key on your keyboard (or click the "Settings" link in the upper-right corner of the screen). The Settings window opens as shown in Figure 9-8. There are only three tabs here: General, Calendars, and Mobile Setup.

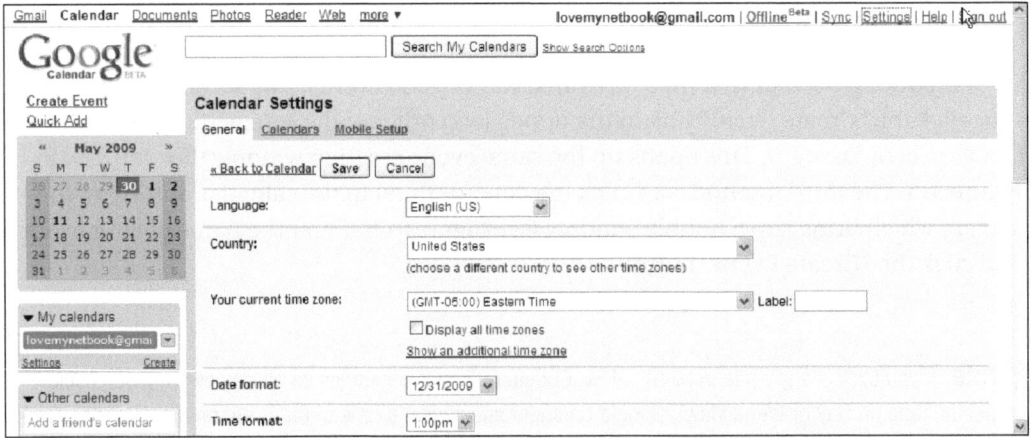

Figure 9-8. *Use the Settings window to create new calendars and tweak settings.*

The General tab lets you modify the way Google Calendar displays times and dates, as well as define the default view (I changed this to Month for the Default View setting), including whether to show weekends on your calendar. Click the "Google Calendar Help" link in the upper-right corner if you wish to learn about each and every setting on this tab, and always remember to click the Save button to keep any changes you've made.

Now click the Calendars tab; the screen changes as shown in Figure 9-9.

Figure 9-9. *The Calendars tab lets you create additional calendars.*

You can create specialty calendars if you click the button called "Create new calendar." I've created one in Figure 9-10 called "Jim's Public Calendar."

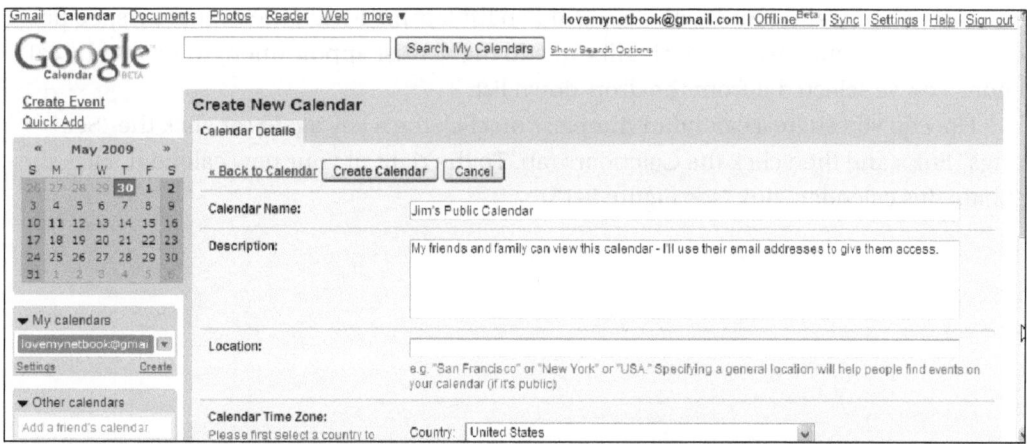

Figure 9-10. *Create a public calendar that others can see on the Internet.*

After entering a description, I click the Create Calendar button. Note the left edge of the screen shown in Figure 9-11: There is now a second item in that list under the My Calendars section. Calendars are color-coded, so appointments made in blue are for my private calendar, while appointments made in red are visible to those whom I give permission to view my calendar (I'll explain how to do that shortly).

Figure 9-11. *You can create multiple calendars that appear in the My Calendars list.*

Now when I create an event, a drop-down list lets me assign the event to a specific calendar (see Figure 9-12). Now I'd like to add the dentist appointment to my public calendar, so I've selected it from the drop-down list.

How do you share a calendar? Simple: You click the S key again (or click the "Settings" link), and then click the Calendars tab. To the right of your new calendar, click the "Share this calendar" link (see Figure 9-13).

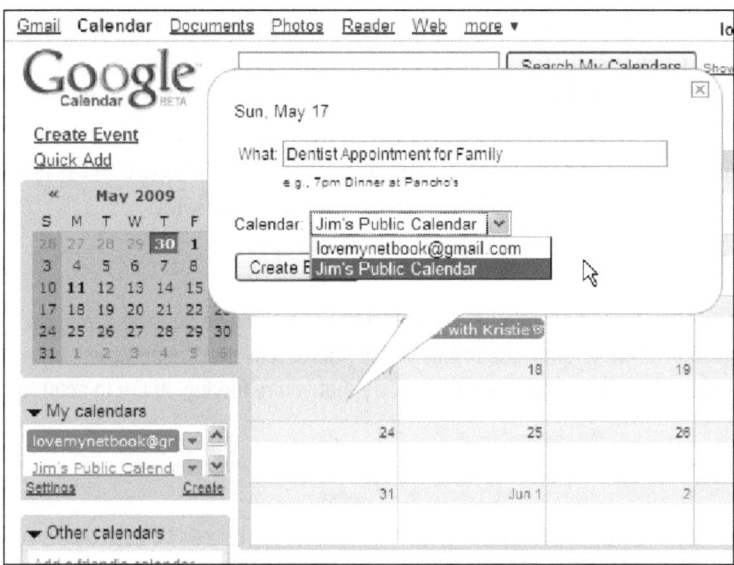

Figure 9-12. *When creating an event, you can specify which calendar will hold it.*

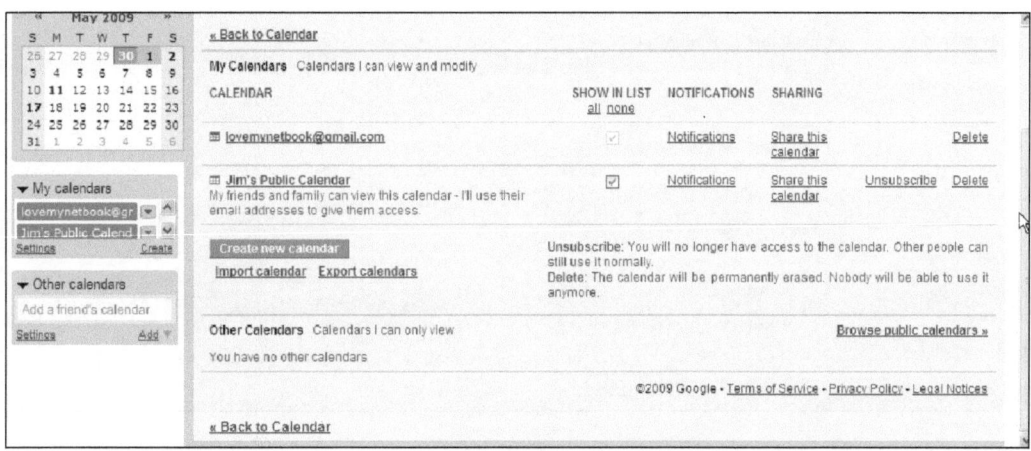

Figure 9-13. *Click on the "Share this Calendar" link to let others see your events.*

This brings up a new screen (see Figure 9-14). You can place a check in the box labeled "Make this calendar public" and everyone in the world will be able to see the events for that particular calendar, which is useful for clubs and organizations that wish to share their upcoming events with the world. For those times when you'd prefer to be more discriminating, however, use the "Share with specific people" section (also seen in Figure 9-14) and provide the email address for each person you wish to give viewing permission.

■**Note**   The email address you provide doesn't have to be a Gmail address, but Google pops up a window asking whether you'd like to invite non-Gmail addressees to join Gmail. Addressees don't need Gmail, but they do need a Google account to access your calendar, so don't worry that you're forcing others to acquire yet another email address.

You can also click the Permission Settings drop-down box in Figure 9-14 and specify whether that person can view, make changes, or even add other names to the list (using the "Make changes AND manage sharing" option).

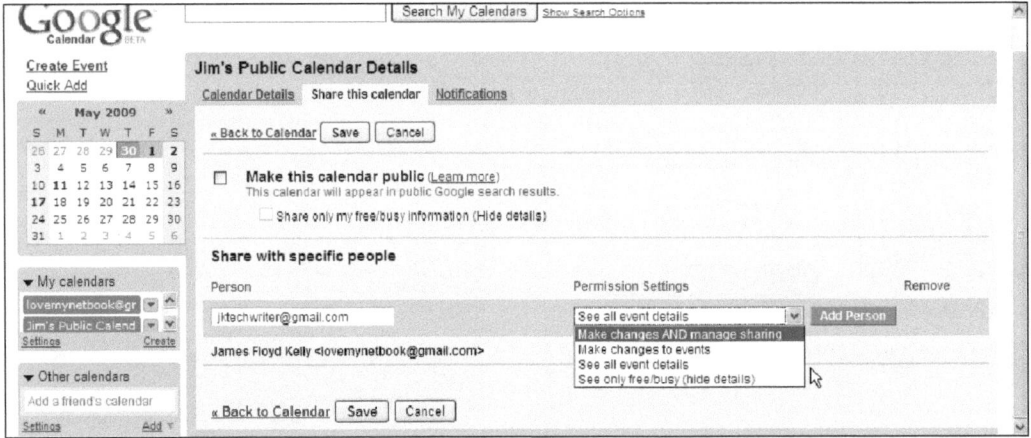

Figure 9-14. *Share a calendar with the world or only certain individuals.*

Click the Add Person button when done; this sends the individual an email (see Figure 9-15) and adds the calendar to that person's Google Calendar screen (see Figure 9-16).

You can find the final feature of Google Calendar that I'd like to show you, Mobile Setup, on the Settings screen. (Note that Google Calendar includes many more interesting features—be sure to click the "Help" link to get a complete tutorial and introduction to other features.)

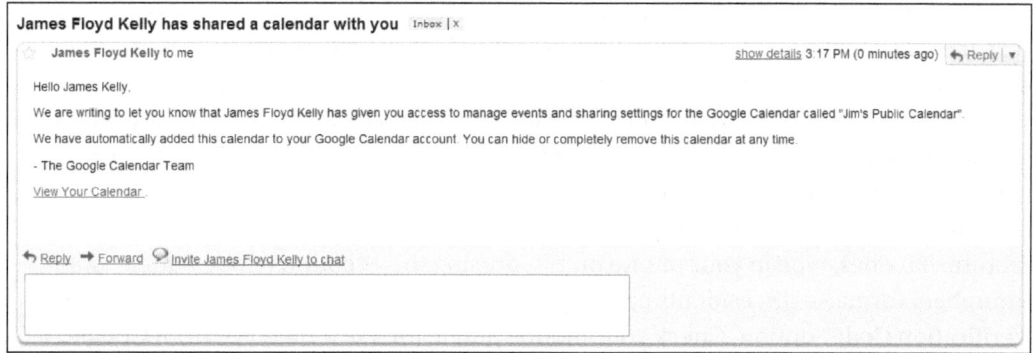

Figure 9-15. *Those invited to view your new calendar can see it on their own Google Calendars.*

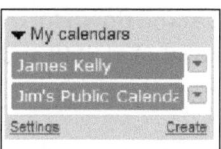

Figure 9-16. *Your calendars are grouped together and color coded.*

Click the "Settings" link or press the S key on your keyboard, and then click the Mobile Setup tab (see Figure 9-17).

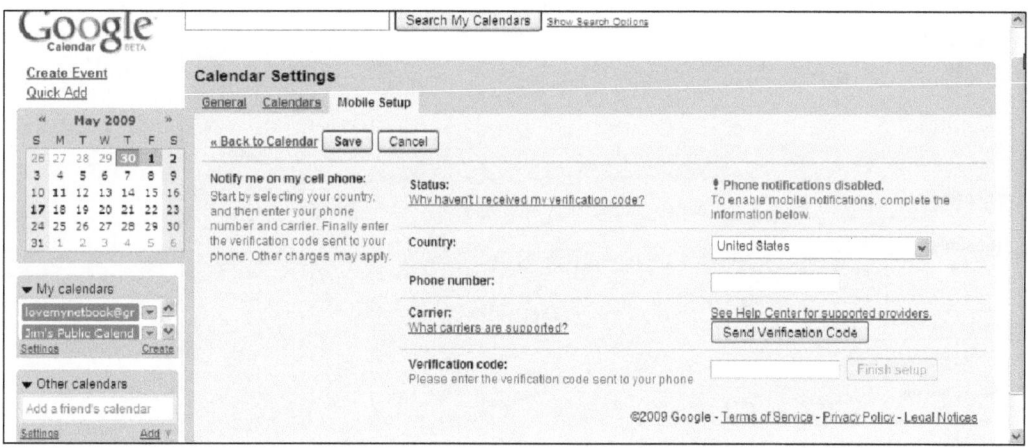

Figure 9-17. *The Mobile Setup screen allows you to receive text message reminders.*

Signing up with this service means you can have Google Calendar send you text-message reminders for your events. You can also have the service add these events and send you text messages for new events to Google Calendar, a nice feature when you don't have your netbook or Internet access, but need to add a new and important appointment. (Note that standard fees for text messages apply here, so check with your mobile-service provider for pricing.)

Click the "What carriers are supported" option to verify your carrier allows this feature. If it does, type in your phone number (using the +<country code><area code> <number> format—US residents can skip the country code portion) and click the "Send Verification Code" option. Check your mobile phone for a text message from Google. Type the code you receive into the Verification Code text box (see Figure 9-17) and click the Finish Setup button. You'll receive another text notifying you that the setup was successful. That's it! Now let's see how it works.

Create a new event as described earlier in the chapter, but this time scroll down to the Options area and click the "Add a reminder" link if you don't see one labeled SMS and select a reminder interval such as "1 hour" (see Figure 9-18).

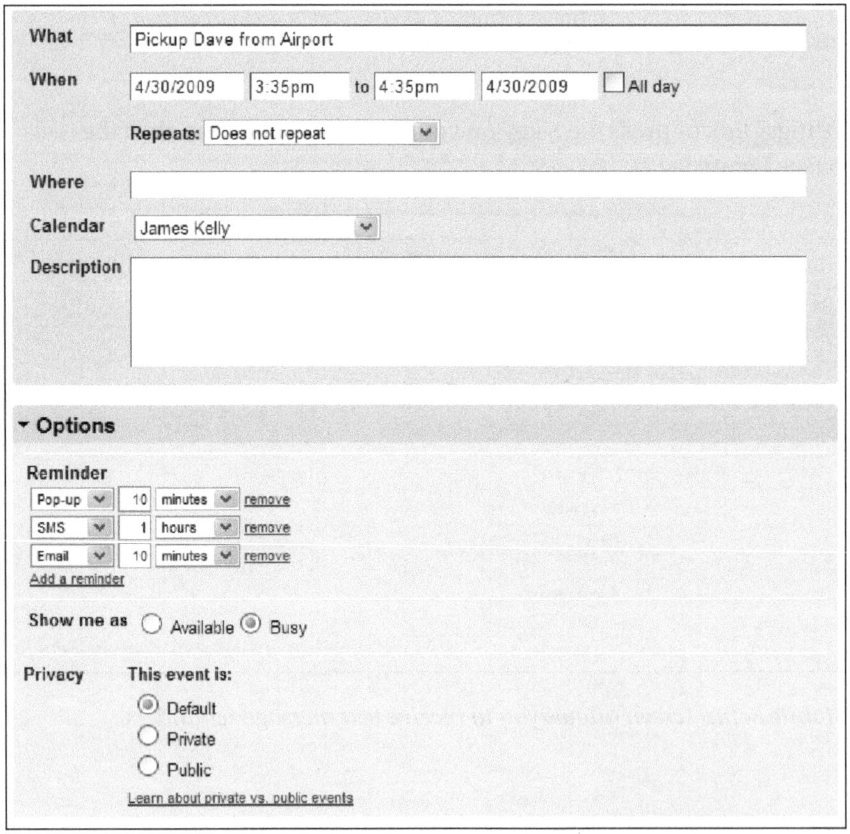

Figure 9-18. *Configure an event to send you a text message (SMS).*

Following these steps sends you a text message after the specified interval elapses (see Figure 9-19).

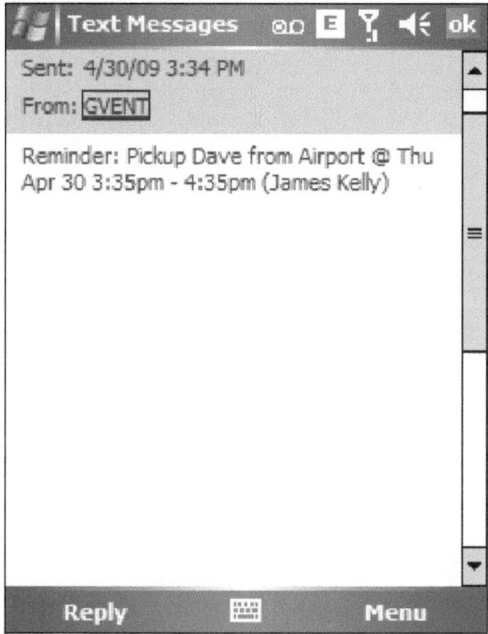

Figure 9-19. *Get a text message reminder on your mobile phone.*

Notice also in Figure 9-18 that you can configure reminder/alerts to be sent via email and as pop-up alerts on your screen. (Keep in mind that the pop-up alerts do require you to have Google Calendar open on your netbook for them to appear.)

I love the way Gmail and Google Calendar work together; I hope the past couple chapters have given you an appreciation of their capabilities, as well. I use both applications for both personal and work situations, and I can't imagine not having access to them—they make my life so much easier, and I'm sure they'll help you, too.

What's Next

Many of the applications I've covered in this book fall under the umbrella of cloud computing; they not only make using your netbook more fun, but also less expensive. In keeping with the trend of finding and using free (or low-cost) software on your netbook, I'd like to show you one of the most popular and well-received set of free Open Source applications, one which you're very likely to find indispensable when it comes to using your netbook. It's called OpenOffice.org, and I think you're going to like it.

CHAPTER 10

■ ■ ■

Netbooks and OpenOffice.org

In Chapter 5 I showed you the collection of productivity apps that Google Docs offers: Document, Spreadsheet, and Presentation. Google Docs is the perfect example of cloud computing; you don't have to install any additional software on your netbook in order to use these three applications.

Google Docs is a great solution for netbook users looking for word processing, spreadsheet, and slideshow software, but it does have its limitations. Google Docs is not as "feature rich" as some applications you might be familiar with, and it's a tricky balance to give users a set of fast and useful features, while also keeping the application free. Google is a business, and it has to make the hard decisions about what to include and what not to include with all of its free cloud computing applications.

If you find Google Docs useful and enjoy the freedom of having your files available from any computer with an Internet connection, then by all means keep using it. But if you've found that one of the Google Docs apps just doesn't offer everything you need—or if you prefer to have your files stored on your own hard drive for security reasons or total accessibility (or both)—then I'd like to introduce you to another option.

In Chapter 4 I introduced you to the concepts of cloud computing and open source. Whereas Google Docs is pure cloud computing, OpenOffice.org is a great example of open source done right. Let's take a look.

OpenOffice.org

OpenOffice.org is both an application and an organization. While it's okay to refer to the software as OpenOffice, the group would really prefer that you call it OpenOffice.org. Microsoft took a dislike to "OpenOffice" a while back, arguing it was too similar to its own product, Office. So the software was renamed OpenOffice.org—problem solved.

OpenOffice.org is a group of software developers who have come together (virtually, via the Web, but also at professional gatherings like developer conferences) to provide an open source (free to use, free to download, free to modify) set of word processor, spreadsheet, and slideshow applications. This group is continually improving the software by fixing bugs (reported by users), adding new features (requested by users), and providing tutorials and help documentation (provided by users). I bet you're seeing a pattern here: part of the success of OpenOffice.org comes from the large user community that has supported this group of developers and the work it is doing.

Together, this group of developers is turning OpenOffice.org into a first class set of productivity applications. The software is free to download (more on this shortly) and install on your netbook right now (see Figure 10-1).

Note As I write this chapter, the latest version of OpenOffice.org is 3.1, but this group of developers doesn't rest, so you might find a newer version by the time you read this. No problem: Updates to OpenOffice.org's apps typically don't change the way the suite looks and operates, so you should find the information in this chapter relevant, even if there is a newer version available.

Rather than tell you what OpenOffice.org offers, however, I'm going to walk you through downloading and installing it in the next section. OpenOffice.org is not a large application (it uses less than 700 MB of hard drive space), and it's easy to uninstall if you find that it isn't for you. So, turn on your netbook, connect to the Internet, and follow along.

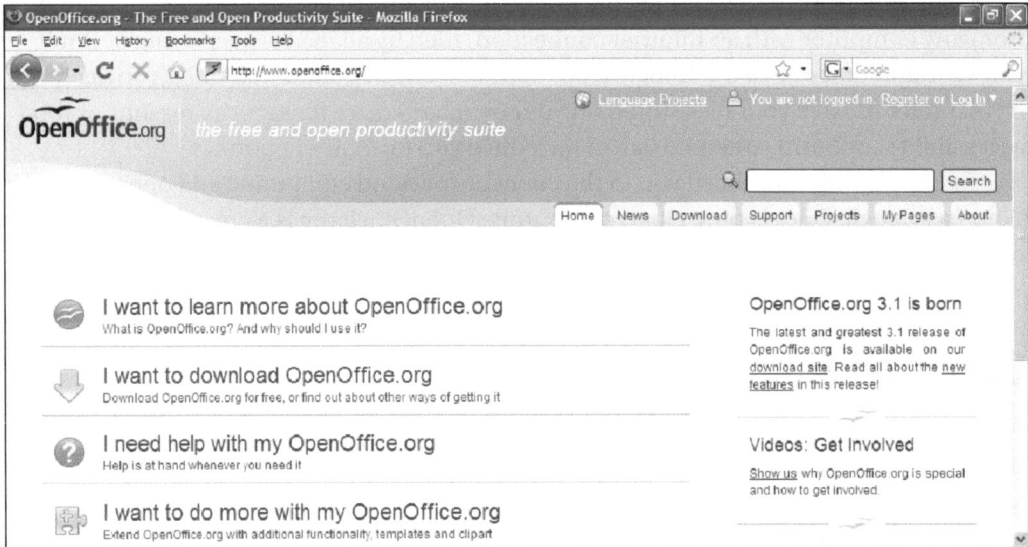

Figure 10-1. *The OpenOffice.org web site is the place to start for downloading or learning about this suite.*

Download and Install OpenOffice.org

Open your web browser to www.openoffice.org and click the "I want to download OpenOffice.org" link shown previously in Figure 10-1. Click the big arrow shown in Figure 10-2 to download the current version of OpenOffice.org for Windows.

Figure 10-2. *Download the Windows version of OpenOffice.org.*

Save the installation file to your computer's hard drive. The download is approximately 150 MB in size, so it shouldn't take too long to download with a high-speed DSL or cable connection. When you're done, double-click the install file (Figure 10-3 shows the Installation Preparation screen that starts the installation process). Click the Next button to continue.

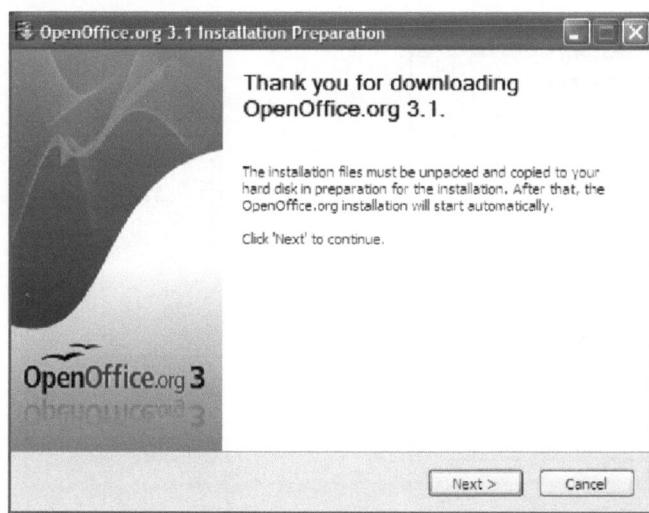

Figure 10-3. *The Installation Preparation screen unpacks the install files.*

This brings up the "Select Folder" screen (see Figure 10-4); I recommend accepting the default installation folder, but click the Browse button if you wish to change the location where the files will be copied. Click the Unpack button to continue.

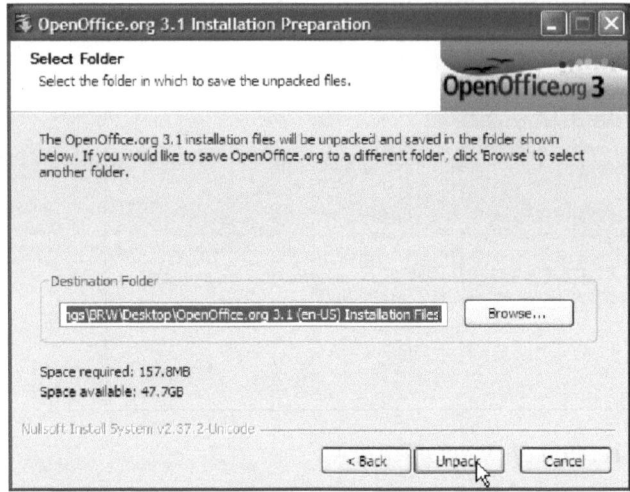

Figure 10-4. *Allow OpenOffice.org to copy files to a default location or change it.*

The next screen is the Installation Wizard welcome screen (see Figure 10-5). Click the Next button to continue.

Figure 10-5. *The Installation Wizard will walk you through the OpenOffice.org installation.*

Now provide your name (and organization name if relevant). You can also choose to allow other user accounts on your netbook to use OpenOffice.org or keep the applications private and for your use only. Click the Next button as shown in Figure 10-6.

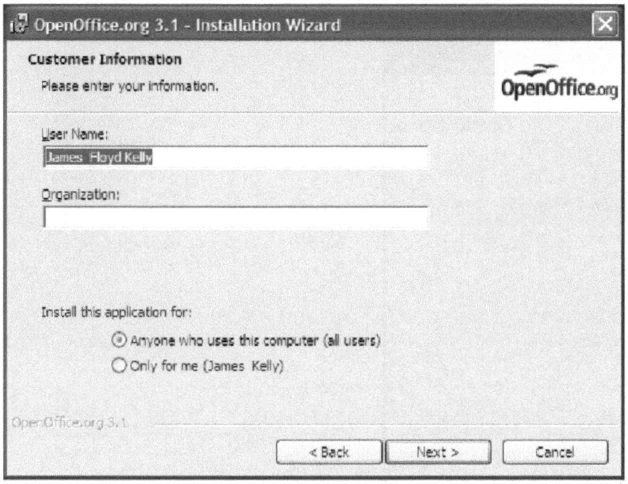

Figure 10-6. *Provide name and organization information.*

Figure 10-7 shows the next screen, where you'll choose whether to install all of the programs included with OpenOffice.org (recommended) or pick and choose only those you need. Click the Custom button if you wish to deselect a program (the spreadsheet program, for example). I recommend installing all the programs at this time; you can always remove a specific program later. Click the Next button to continue.

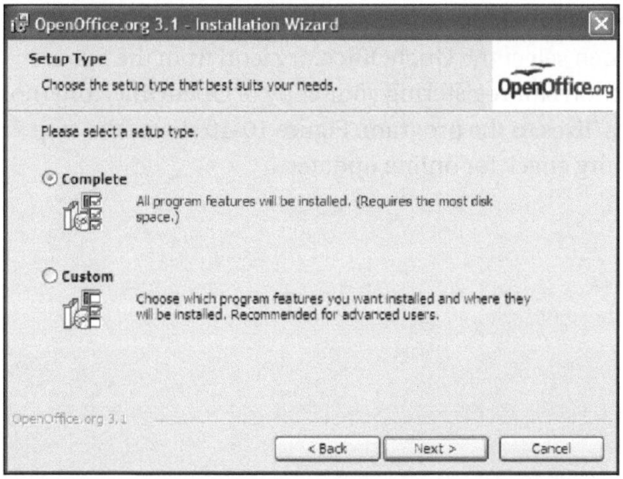

Figure 10-7. *Select a Complete or Custom installation.*

Now you're ready to begin the installation; click the Install button as shown in Figure 10-8 to finish installing OpenOffice.org or click the Back button to make any changes. You can also uncheck the box labeled "Create a start link on desktop" if you don't want a shortcut icon added to the desktop.

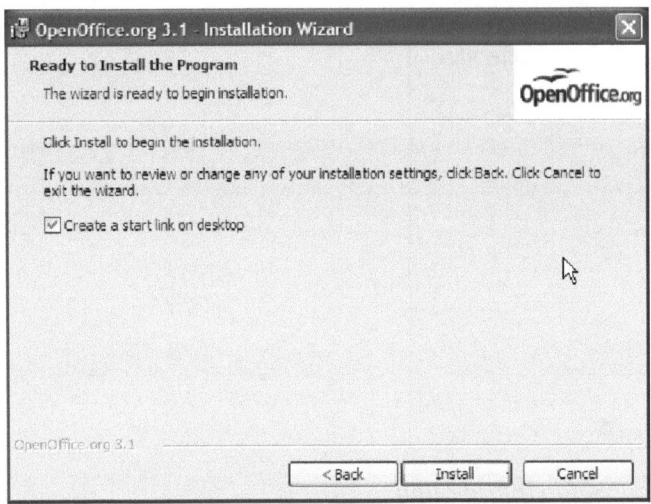

Figure 10-8. *OpenOffice.org is ready to install.*

OpenOffice.org will begin copying its files to your netbook. This installation is fairly quick and takes only a few minutes. When the installation completes, you should see a screen similar to the one shown in Figure 10-9. Click the Finish button to close the screen.

If you allowed OpenOffice.org to place a shortcut icon on your desktop, go ahead and double-click it. (If you don't have the shortcut icon, click Start, then All Programs/ Programs, OpenOffice.org 3.1, and then select the OpenOffice.org icon from the flyout menu.) Follow the on-screen instructions for registering your copy of OpenOffice.org (not required) and download any updates/fixes to the program. Figure 10-10 shows the step where I've elected to let OpenOffice.org check for online updates.

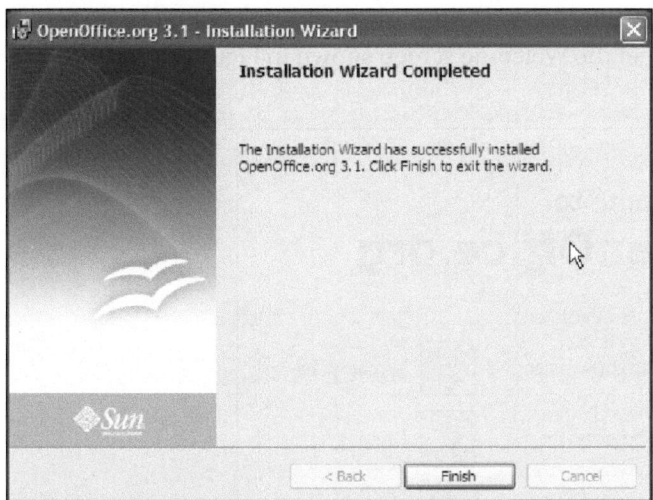

Figure 10-9. *The Installation Wizard is finished, and OpenOffice.org is ready to go.*

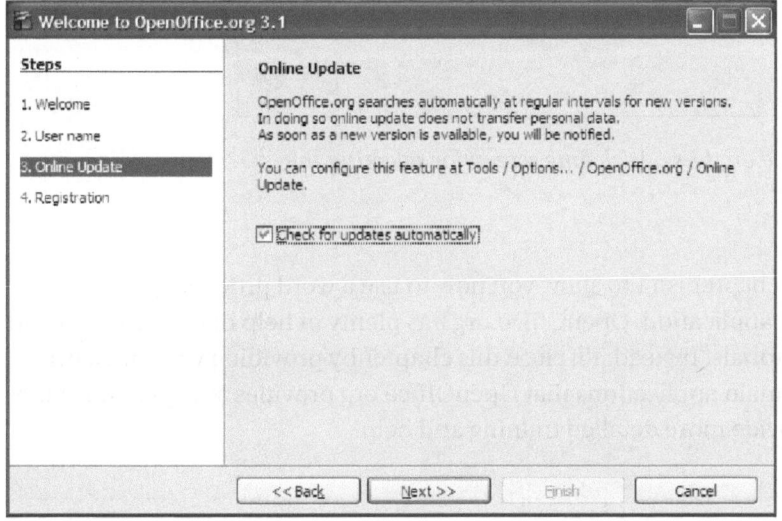

Figure 10-10. *Let OpenOffice.org search for updates online automatically.*

After turning on the ability that allows OpenOffice.org to check for online updates and registering my installation, I get the Welcome screen shown in Figure 10-11.

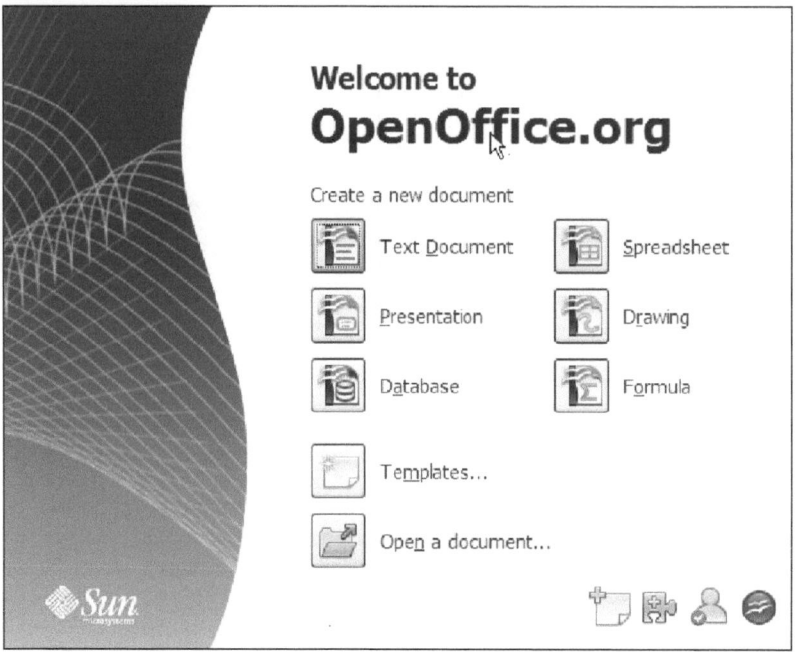

Figure 10-11. *OpenOffice.org has a Welcome screen for selecting the program I wish to use.*

My goal with this chapter isn't to show you how to use a word processor, spreadsheet, or presentation application. OpenOffice.org has plenty of help documentation and built-in and online tutorials. Instead, I'll close this chapter by providing you with a brief overview of the three main applications that OpenOffice.org provides and give you some web sites that can provide more detailed training and help.

■**Note** OpenOffice also includes additional applications: a database program, a vector-graphics program (called Draw), and a math-equation tool called Math. You can access all of the OpenOffice.org programs using the shortcut icon on your desktop or by browsing the OpenOffice.org list of programs found under the Start button.

Let's start by clicking the "Text Document" seen in Figure 10-11; this document opens Writer, the OpenOffice.org word processor.

OpenOffice.org Writer

Writer is the OpenOffice.org word processing application. When you first open a new text document, you get a blank screen similar to the one shown in Figure 10-12.

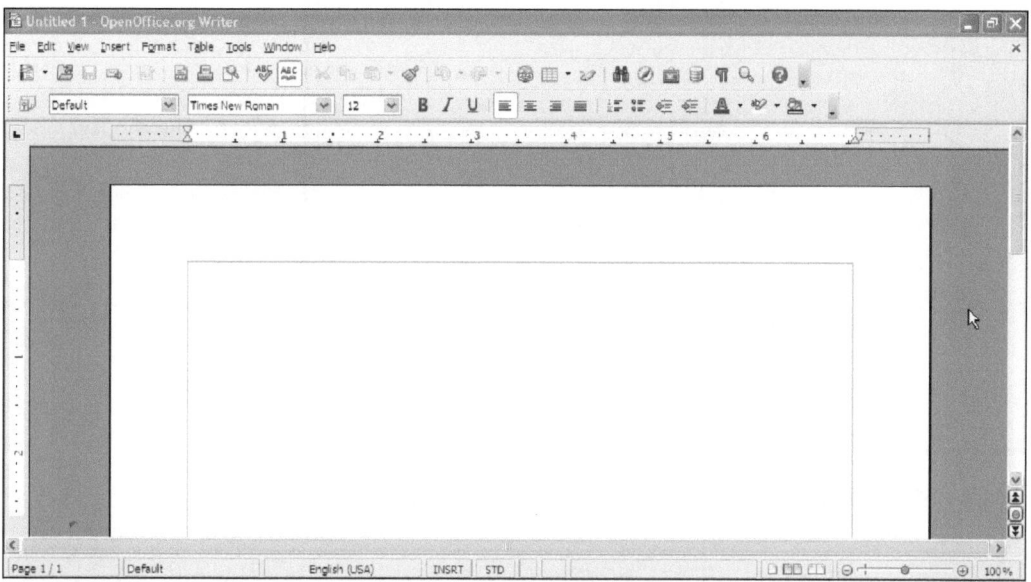

Figure 10-12. *A Writer document with toolbars and a blank page.*

Along the top of the screen are standard menus, such as File, Edit, Format, and Tools. Below the menus are the two toolbars that contain buttons allowing you to print, save, format text, and change fonts, among other tasks. (If you hover your mouse pointer over a button for a moment, a small bit of text pops up to tell you that button's function.)

Writer is a full-featured word processor, fully compatible with Microsoft Office's competing product, Word. Although the default file extension used by Writer is .odt, you can save your document in many different formats, including the .doc format used by earlier versions of Word. Other options, shown in Figure 10-13, include HTML, .txt (basic text), and .sdw. The last file format is for StarOffice Writer, a word processor based on Writer that is overseen by Sun Microsystems. StarOffice Writer is part of the StarOffice suite, a productivity package based on the OpenOffice.org product that offers additional built-in features not found in OpenOffice.org.

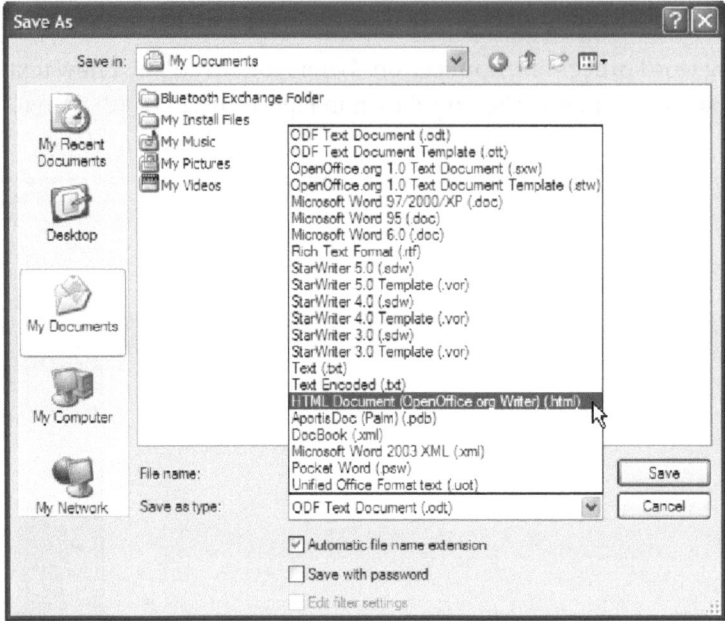

Figure 10-13. *Documents can be saved in formats other than .odt.*

Writer is one of the most popular programs included with OpenOffice.org. Many users enjoy using it because of its speed; it opens quickly, saves fast, and shuts down even faster. One of the benefits of Writer's uncluttered user interface is that it avoids the "bloat" found in other word processors. Writer is improving with every new version of OpenOffice.org.

But Writer isn't the only program that's popular. Close down Writer, double-click the desktop shortcut icon, and click "Spreadsheet" (refer back to Figure 10-11) to take a look at Calc, the OpenOffice.org spreadsheet application.

OpenOffice.org Calc

Calc is the OpenOffice.org spreadsheet application shown in Figure 10-14.

Like Writer, Calc has a range of menus and toolbars that offer most of the basic options you'll find useful with a spreadsheet application. Calc can open Microsoft Excel spreadsheets, as well as save spreadsheets you create with the .xls file format. (The default OpenOffice.org Calc file extension is .ods.)

If you're familiar with other spreadsheet applications, you've probably seen graphics such as pie charts and bar charts typically created using these kinds of programs. Calc has the same functionality and provides a Chart Wizard (see Figure 10-15) that can help you create some eye-catching charts from the spreadsheet's data.

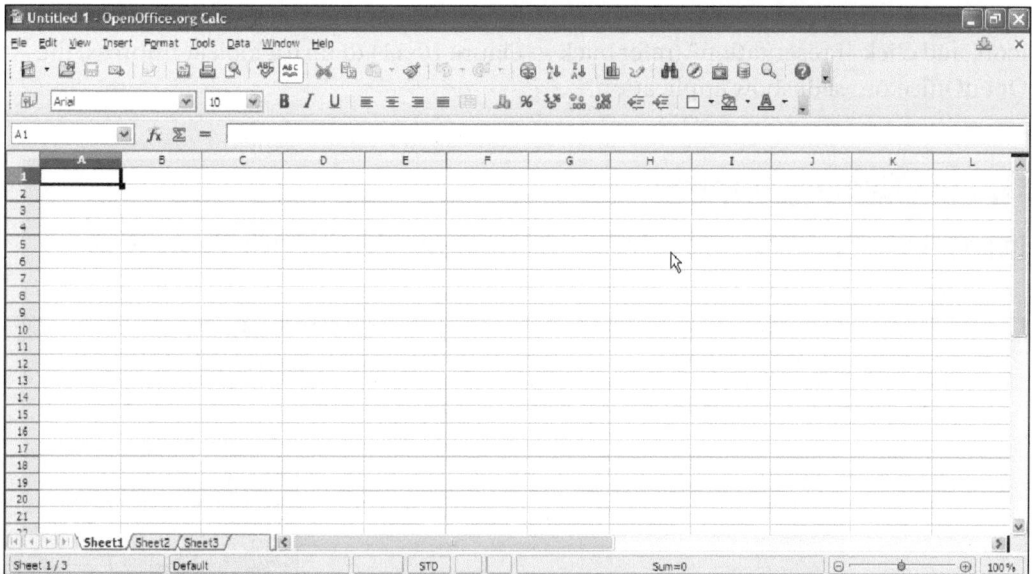

Figure 10-14. *Calc is a full-featured spreadsheet program that comes free with OpenOffice.org.*

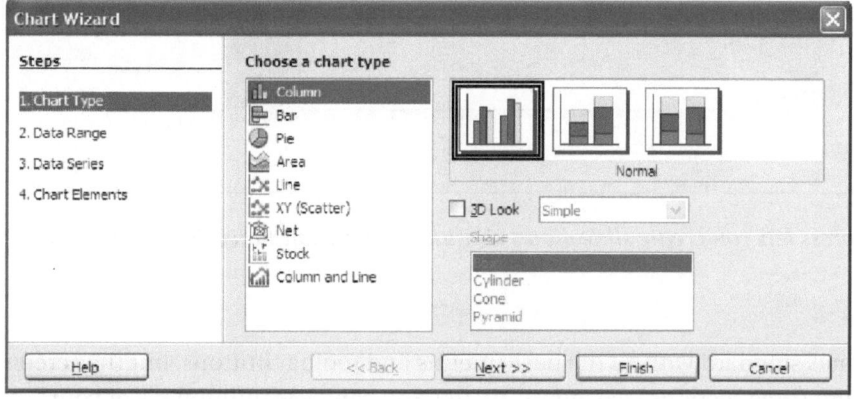

Figure 10-15. *A Chart Wizard can create all kinds of colorful and eye-catching charts.*

Calc has a solid reputation for being one of the most well-developed programs in the OpenOffice.org collection of applications. Writer doesn't have nearly the number of features found in Word, but users of Calc often find it to be competitive with Microsoft Excel's list of useful features.

Go ahead and close down Calc, double-click the OpenOffice.org desktop shortcut icon, and click "Presentation" (refer back to Figure 10-11) to take a look at Impress, the OpenOffice.org slideshow application.

OpenOffice.org Impress

Impress is the OpenOffice.org slideshow design application shown in Figure 10-16.

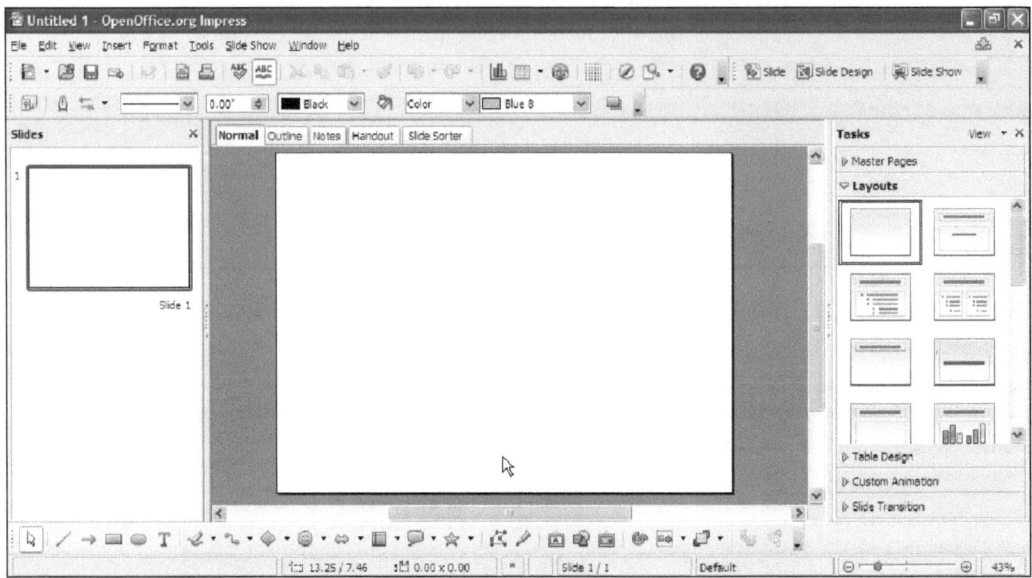

Figure 10-16. *Impress lets you create slideshows similar to Microsoft PowerPoint or Apple Keynote.*

Impress comes standard with all the basic menus and toolbar buttons, but the screen is also divided into three sections (see Figure 10-16). You can view thumbnails of your slides along the left side of the screen, modify the current slide in the center window, and select various layouts and special animations from the right side of the screen.

Impress can open Microsoft PowerPoint slideshows, as well as save the slideshows you create with the .ppt file format (see in Figure 10-17). Note that the default OpenOffice. org Impress file extension is .odp.

Together, Writer, Calc, and Impress provide you with three powerful tools that you're sure to find useful. If you're unfamiliar with how to use any or all of these applications, OpenOffice.org provides some of the best help documentation you can find, including tutorials, at http://support.openoffice.org (see Figure 10-18).

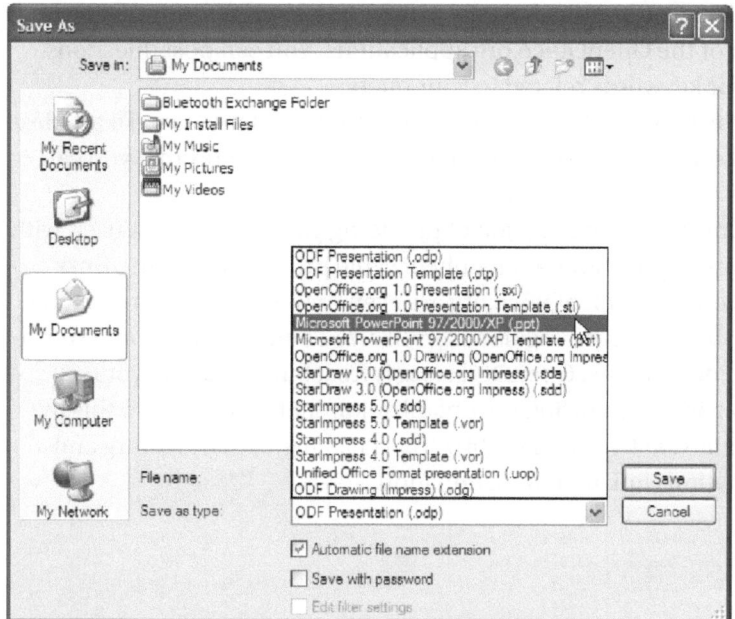

Figure 10-17. *You can save Impress slideshows using the .ppt PowerPoint format.*

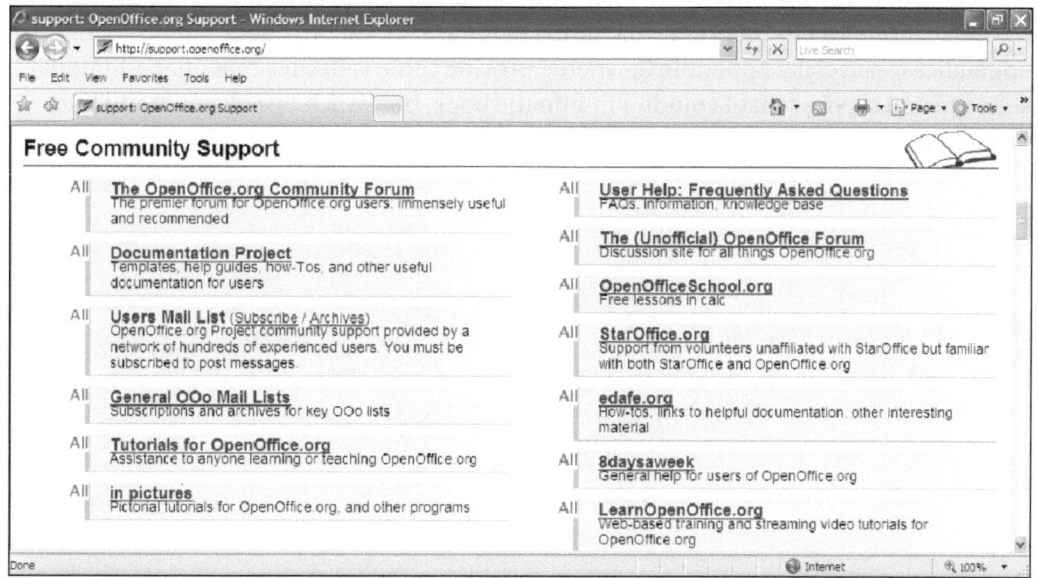

Figure 10-18. *Free help is available via the OpenOffice community support forums.*

Click the "OpenOffice.org Community Forum" listing, and you'll find specific forum discussion groups for each of the OpenOffice.org applications. You can post questions, read answers, and search for keywords related to your query.

Scattered around the forum you'll find tutorials submitted by users, How-To articles that provide details on performing all sorts of special tasks, and templates that you can download to give your files a more polished look.

OpenOffice.org has done an outstanding job of providing you, the netbook user, with three of the best productivity applications at an unbelievable price: free. But the work doesn't stop, and the developers of OpenOffice.org are even now adding features, fixing bugs, and improving the software—even regular users like you and me can submit tutorials and contribute How-To documents. OpenOffice.org is free, but if you find yourself using it a lot, you might consider supporting the organization that creates it. Do this by making a donation of any amount by visiting `http://contributing.openoffice.org` and clicking the Monetary Donations link to make a donation.

What's Next

We haven't even begun to scratch the surface of what software and services are available for your netbook. Netbook sales continue to grow, so you can expect more companies to find ways to make cloud computing services available for this new class of computers. Open source is also growing every year, with new groups focusing on providing quality applications for all computers, including netbooks. Be sure to check out this book's appendices, especially Appendix C, where I provide some web sites that offer additional software and services that I couldn't fit into the book, but which I think you'll still find very useful.

APPENDIX A

■ ■ ■

Netbook Manufacturers

The following is by no means a comprehensive list of every company that sells netbooks. As netbooks grow in popularity, expect more companies to begin offering more models with even more variations on the available hardware and software.

In addition to the list of companies provided in this appendix, be sure to check out this comparison webpage that is updated regularly; a large assortment of netbooks is coming out of China, and many buyers are not familiar with some of these companies so the comparison list might be useful to you.

http://en.wikipedia.org/wiki/Comparison_of_netbooks

- Dell: www.dell.com (currently the Dell Mini 9, Dell Mini 10, and Dell Mini 12 are available)

- HP: www.hp.com (search the company's web site for "Hp Mini")

- Asus: http://eeepc.asus.com (netbooks are the company's specialty)

- Acer: http://eeepc.asus.com (search for "Aspire One")

- Lenovo: http://shop.lenovo.com (search for "S Series")

- MSI: www.msimobile.com (search for "Wind")

- Samsung: www.samsung.com (unusual model names, so do a simple search for "netbook")

Be sure to check out the following blogs for discussions, hands-on reviews, and news on upcoming netbook models:

- www.netbookera.com

- http://netbookblog.info

APPENDIX B

Upgrading a Netbook to Windows 7

There is good news and bad news when it comes to Windows 7 and netbooks.

First, the good news: A version of Windows 7 has been designed specifically for low-power devices such as netbooks, and early tests (including one performed by your author) are impressive. I won't need convincing to run Windows 7 on my netbook.

Second, the bad news: If you're running Windows XP on your current netbook, there is no Windows 7 upgrade product (sold at a lower price). Windows XP is not designed to be upgraded, which means you need to purchase a full version of Windows 7 and perform a clean installation on your netbook.

Fortunately, you have a handful of options:

- Stick with Windows XP on your netbook—yes, it's an older operating system, but if it works, why rock the boat? If you don't need to install any cutting-edge software on your netbook that requires Windows 7, then consider sticking with XP until your netbook goes out in a blaze of glory.

- Give Ubuntu a try! Many netbook owners are finding that Ubuntu (Linux) is a stable little operating system that's perfect for these devices. Ubuntu has even created a special version of the operating system called Ubuntu Netbook Remix that features lower hardware requirements, including lower hard-drive space. You can download it for free by visiting www.ubuntu.com; once you download it, visit https://help.ubuntu.com/community/Installation/FromImgFiles for instructions on installing Ubuntu on your netbook using either a CD or a Flash drive. For more information on Ubuntu, check out my book, *Ubuntu on a Dime: The Path to Low-Cost Computing* (Apress, 2009).

- If you have a DVD drive that connects to your netbook via USB, you can purchase the full version of Windows 7 and follow the included instructions for preparing your netbook's hard drive and installing the new operating system.

- If you do not have a DVD drive, however, don't fret. Many tutorials are popping up all over the Internet that explain how to install Windows 7 on a netbook using nothing more than a USB Flash drive. I've found two great tutorials, one a video and one text-based. Keep in mind that these instructions might or might not apply to your specific model of netbook. I suggest a Google search of "install Windows 7 netbook *<your model name/number>*" and see what shows up. Regardless, the following resources should give you a good idea of what upgrading to Windows 7 on your netbook involves:

Video: `http://edge.technet.com/Media/Installing-Win7-using-a-USB-Stick`

Web page: `www.liliputing.com/2009/05/guide-for-installing-windows-7-on-most-netbooks.html`

I hope you find this wide range of links useful. I also recommend that you check out Microsoft's official Windows 7 site at `www.microsoft.com/windows7`.

Additional Netbook Apps to Consider

There are many great applications out there that are perfect for a netbook user. While these apps are also useful for other types of computers, netbooks stand to benefit the most from these applications because of their smaller hard drives, built-in WiFi and web cams, and enhanced portability. Not all of these applications rely on the cloud computing paradigm, but most of them do fall into that category.

These are just some of my favorite applications for netbooks that I've used (or continue to use); however, this list is by no means exhaustive. Perform a Google search for "cloud computing apps" and you're sure to find many more.

Mozy

www.mozy.com: Backing up your netbook data is one of the most important tasks you can perform on a regular basis (add scanning for viruses to that list, too). But backing up your data to another folder just doesn't make sense—what if your netbook is stolen or damaged? Backing up your data to CD or DVD is a better solution, but all too frequently people lose them, the CDs or DVDs get scratched, or the media are stored in the same home or office as the netbook. What if there's a fire?

A better solution for backing up data is to store it in a completely separate location. That's where Mozy comes in; you can sign up for a free 2GB (gigabyte) account and move files over to Mozy's backup hard drives using a simple-to-use software tool that you download and install on your netbook. If you should ever delete a file accidentally (or your netbook is stolen or damaged), Mozy can get you back your files quickly and easily. You might find (as I have) that the $4.95 per month fee for unlimited storage is well worth the cost. I currently have more than 20GB of data backed up using this service, including photos, videos, book chapters, and more. If my netbook's hard drive dies tomorrow, I can get it all back. (From one netbook user to another: If you choose only one application from this list to use with your netbook, this should be the one.)

Doodle

www.doodle.com: Have you ever tried to get three or more friends to agree on a movie, including a place and a time? Have you ever tried to organize a birthday party and getting RSVPs, so you can figure out how much food to prepare? Doodle is a nice little service that I use frequently to make these kinds of decisions. It's free; I log in, pick the potential dates and times that I'm considering for hosting a get together or seeing a movie, and I enter the email addresses of all those I wish to invite. Each person invited can click a link in the email he receives and click the dates and times that work best for him; the results are tallied in real-time, so my guests and I can view the voting results. Doodle works great for finding the date and time for a planned event that works best for the most people. You can also use Doodle to help with scheduling meetings, conference calls, school events, and other activities where it's important to get the most people involved.

Skype

www.skype.com: I have a young son who loves to see and talk to his grandparents. Unfortunately, the grandparents live in different states, and my son is too young to understand how to use a phone. Fortunately I have my netbook, broadband Internet, a web cam—and Skype. Skype is a free service that lets you make voice or video phone calls to other Skype users at no cost. All it requires is a small application that's installed on your netbook and an Internet connection (dial-up will support voice only, while video requires a broadband connection, such as DSL or Cable). If your netbook has a built-in web cam and microphone like mine (or a headset, which costs around $20-$30), you're ready to go. My son's grandparents have web cams and microphones installed on their computers, which means my son can see and hear them speaking to him. This is a great tool for work and home. Skype lets you talk and/or see other Skype users that you've added to your list of contacts—even overseas contacts. For example, I use Skype frequently to speak with one of my editors who lives in London! The cost of a phone call would be enormous, but Skype lets me chat away, using the Internet as my carrier, completely free.

Print What You Like

www.printwhatyoulike.com: When I'm writing a book, I frequently find a lot of useful information on web sites that I'd prefer to print out and keep in a folder. Unfortunately, a lot of web sites have "other stuff" that I'd rather not print, including advertisements, comments left by readers, graphics that I don't need, and so on. It's a bit aggravating to need to print two or three paragraphs of information and have my printer eject three or four pages of non-relevant content. That's why I love Print What You Like (PWYL). I simply enter the URL (web site address) of the sites I want to print, and PWYL lets me choose what I'd like to remove from the final printout. After I remove the pictures, advertisements and other flotsam, I can even save the final result as a PDF to my hard drive. The service is 100% free. Note that there is a paid version that provides additional features, but I'm still using the free online version (with no software installed on my netbook), and I haven't yet found a reason to upgrade my account so far. Print What You Like is a great way to save paper, money, and time, so be sure to give it a test.

Facebook

`www.facebook.com`: A recent statistic I read said that one in five Internet users has a Facebook account, so it's very likely that you're already familiar with Facebook if you're a netbook owner. Facebook has changed the way that people stay in contact with their friends, family, and coworkers. It's also proved extremely popular with helping people to track down long-lost friends because the service includes a search feature that makes it easy to find and send a quick, "Are you the John Smith I knew at Florida State University in 1992?" Facebook allows you to upload pictures and videos, as well as view the same content that your friends post. You can easily configure Facebook so strangers can't view your information unless you "Friend" them; this means you've been contacted by them (or they've been contacted by you), and a mutual agreement to be friends has been reached. Once you have a list of friends—a list that seems to grow and grow, by the way—you'll be able to read about their activities, view their pictures and videos, and leave comments on their pages. They can do the same for you. It might sound like an exaggeration, but Facebook is changing the way that people communicate and stay in touch with each other. If you haven't tried it, it's free to sign up and use, and using it doesn't require that you install any software.

Google Sites

`http://sites.google.com`: The typical method for creating a public web site also includes paying for the software to create the web site and paying a hosting service to make the files available to anyone who visits `www.yourgreatandwonderfulwebsite.com`. Well, Google has another option for you: you can use its free Sites service to create not only your web site, but also pay nothing for Google to host it. All the design tools you need are made available from within your web browser. Simply log in to the Google Sites service, read through a few brief tutorials, and you'll be creating a web site in no time. Google offers various templates, color schemes, and page designs that can be modified easily once you get the hang of using the service. I use the service frequently when I need to create a quick web site for a book or hobby that I'd like to share with others; I can have a web site up and running in less than 30 minutes and share the web address with friends and colleagues. (If you'd like to see an example of one of my Sites, visit `http://sites.google.com/site/priusupgrade`; this site covers how a friend of mine and I converted a Toyota Prius to a plug-in car!)

Mint.com

`www.mint.com`: You might be familiar with personal financial software such as Quicken or Microsoft Money, but Mint.com is a service you should definitely check out. It's a free online money-management service that allows you to manage your bank accounts, investments, and loans. Best of all, it's secure, and your bank most likely has a relationship with Mint.com. The service makes its money from the banks and financial institutions that you choose to monitor with the service; the banks and financial services pay a small fee to Mint.com, so there's no cost to you. Mint.com can help you organize your spending and see where your money is going. It can also help you organize your loans to determine which you should pay off first. You can also configure Mint.com to email you (or send text messages) when large or suspicious charges have been made to your credit cards. Mint.com doesn't know anything more about you than your email address and your zip code; all information related to your accounts is encrypted with the same level of security that banks use (read more at `www.mint.com/privacy/security-tech`). Additional features include the ability to check Mint.com from a mobile phone, create a budget, and create and print graphs and charts to help you understand your overall financial situation. Remember, Mint.com is free, so give it a try.

Hard Drive Imaging

`www.runtime.org/driveimage-xml.htm`: Your hard drive contains the operating system, any applications you've installed, and all your personal files, including photos, music, documents, and more. But even if you back up your data to CD/DVD or an online backup service (see the previously mentioned `www.mozy.com`), a crashed hard drive can still be a major inconvenience because you must reinstall Windows and all your applications. Fortunately, there's a better way: you can create a drive image. Think of a drive image as a photograph of your hard drive that is copied onto CDs or DVDs. Should your hard drive fail (or maybe your netbook catches a really nasty and destructive virus), you just copy the image onto a new hard drive (or the existing one) and you're back to work—there's no need to reinstall the operating system or your applications. Be aware, however, that burning a hard drive image to CDs or DVDs can take some time, depending on the size of your hard drive. I create an image of my hard drive once per quarter; this process typically takes a few hours and requires about seven or eight blank DVDs. To accomplish this, I use a free application called DriveImage XML, which works great. Download, install it, and run it regularly to create hassle-free reinstalls.

Online Photo Editing

www.picnik.com: There are a ton of free photo-editing applications out there, but check out Picnik if you're looking for a nice one that you can use via your web browser. You don't have to register for an account—just visit the site and click the "Get Started Now" button. You browse your hard drive for a photo you wish to edit (registering lets you upload five photos at a time instead of just one at a time) and use the various menus available to remove red eye, crop, rotate, resize, sharpen, and more. When you're done, you can save the edited photo back to your own hard drive or share it with friends and family using supported services such as Flickr, Twitter, or Facebook.

Index

You Need the Companion eBook

Your purchase of this book entitles you to buy the companion PDF-version eBook for only $10. Take the weightless companion with you anywhere.

We believe this Apress title will prove so indispensable that you'll want to carry it with you everywhere, which is why we are offering the companion eBook (in PDF format) for $10 to customers who purchase this book now. Convenient and fully searchable, the PDF version of any content-rich, page-heavy Apress book makes a valuable addition to your programming library. You can easily find and copy code—or perform examples by quickly toggling between instructions and the application. Even simultaneously tackling a donut, diet soda, and complex code becomes simplified with hands-free eBooks!

Once you purchase your book, getting the $10 companion eBook is simple:

❶ Visit **www.apress.com/promo/tendollars/**.

❷ Complete a basic registration form to receive a randomly generated question about this title.

❸ Answer the question correctly in 60 seconds, and you will receive a promotional code to redeem for the $10.00 eBook.

2855 TELEGRAPH AVENUE | SUITE 600 | BERKELEY, CA 94705

Offer valid through 2/2010.